Dear Reneta & family

Thanks for feeding
us yet again!

All our love

Lizzie & Carlo
x

Martha
STEWART'S
MENUS
for ENTERTAINING

Martha
STEWART'S
MENUS
for ENTERTAINING

Photographs by DANA GALLAGHER

Design by ROBERT VALENTINE INCORPORATED

EBURY PRESS
LONDON

✳

To my mother, Martha Kostyra, on the occasion of her eightieth birthday

First published 1994

1 3 5 7 9 10 8 6 4 2

Copyright © 1994 by Martha Stewart
Photographs © 1994 by Dana Gallagher

First published in the United Kingdom in 1994 by
Ebury Press Limited
Random House, 20 Vauxhall Bridge Road, London SW1V 2SA

Random House Australia Pty Limited
20 Alfred Street, Milsons Point, Sydney, New South Wales 2061, Australia

Random House New Zealand Limited
18 Poland Road, Glenfield, Auckland 10, New Zealand

Random House South Africa (Pty) Limited
PO Box 337, Bergvlei, South Africa

Random House UK Limited Reg. No. 954009

Published by arrangement with Clarkson N. Potter, Inc.
201 East 50th Street, New York, New York 10022.

A CIP catalogue record for this book is available from the British Library

ISBN 0 09 179009 3

Printed in Japan

Acknowledgments

Many talented friends and associates contributed their knowledge and time to *Menus for Entertaining* and I would like to thank all of them for making this a most pleasurable experience. ✳ Zacki Murphy helped with several of these chapters, but it was her collaboration on the North Carolina Barbecue that is most indicative of her talent as a fine country cook. Good luck to her with her new restaurant in New York, Zacki's P.B.Q. Salli LaGrone, too, is a fine and careful cook, and she visited Connecticut from her home in Nashville to work with me on the "Fried Green Tomatoes" Brunch menu. Dero Puckett, from Jackson, Mississippi, inspired several menus, and my friends Lily Pei and Marie Mendez offered wonderful ideas and recipes from their native homelands. ✳ Many warm thanks go to Kathy Oberman, who assisted me tirelessly with the shopping, cooking, styling, and recording of these menus. Necy Fernandes, who has worked on almost all my books, proffered advice, style, and recipes from her native Brazil. Roberta "Birdi" Kins and Corey Tippin worked on my first book, and they helped again with this one. Frances Boswell, Dora Ferreyra, Karen Tack, and Louise Burbridge worked in the kitchen as well, styling and cooking with flair and expertise. ✳ Rita Christiansen, Carolyn Kelly, Judy Morris, Susan Varga, Parry Grogan, and Larry Kennedy offered office help and shopping expertise, while Renato Abreu and Renaldo Abreu grew the lovely flowers and vegetables that appear in many of the photographs. ✳ I would also like to thank my friends who loaned me their homes and beaches: Ben and Bonnie Krupinski, Mort Zuckerman, and Jerry and Judy Della Femina. ✳ Thanks and love to my daughter, Alexis, who critiqued and tasted, and loaned me some of her collections for photographs. And gratitude to my friend Susan Magrino for her encouragement, insight, and inspiration. ✳ Many thanks to the staff of Clarkson Potter for their dedicated efforts to get this book to the printer on time: to my new editor, Annetta Hanna, for her gentle and careful editing; to Howard Klein and Jane Treuhaft for their art direction; to my excellent friends Teresa Nicholas and Ed Otto, who worked so hard with Toppan, the printer, to achieve the elegant look and feel of this book; to Copy Chief Mark McCauslin and Executive Managing Editor Laurie Stark for their careful supervision of editing and scheduling; to Sam Chapnick, Etya Pinker Novik, Janet McDonald, Pam Krauss, Katie Workman, and Chesie Hortenstine; to Clarkson Potter's Editorial Director, Lauren Shakely, for her helpful advice; to Crown's Publisher and President, Michelle Sidrane, for her constant encouragement and camaraderie; and to Alberto Vitale, the Chairman and CEO of Random House. ✳ Most important, I offer my sincerest thanks and gratitude to the young woman who photographed everything so exquisitely, Dana Gallagher. With her assistants, Marty Hyers and Beatriz Martins deCosta, she accomplished true magic. And enormous thanks to Robert Valentine and his staff of extraordinary designers—Dina Dell'Arciprete-Hauser, Pamela Hunt-Thomas, and Wayne Wolf—who worked with Dana's photographs to create a lucid and evocative design of great originality.

Contents

Introduction

Things have changed so very much since I wrote my first book, *Entertaining*. Even though I was a working mother in 1982, I baked my own French bread two or three times a week, made pound after pound of *sweet* butter pâte feuilletée, and pressed by hand virtually hundreds of tiny tart shells to be *baked* and filled for hors d'oeuvres and desserts. Obviously I spent an inordinate amount of time in the kitchen, creating, cooking, and preparing for *family* and *guests*. ✳ Nowadays I still want to *entertain*, I still want to cook, but my available time for devising menus, shopping for ingredients, and actual cooking is much more limited. Luckily for me, there has been a general relaxation in home entertaining, a great simplification in *menu* structuring, a less strenuous approach to *table settings* and decoration, and an easing of formality. ✳ This shift from the formal to the relaxed is reflected in *Menus for Entertaining*. Although I've worked on this book for a little over a year, I actually started writing it the moment *Entertaining* was completed. I began compiling *new ideas*, new concepts, and new recipes that would complement the first book without any duplication. I taught seminars using ingredients, *cooking methods*, and table decorating ideas that were different from those I shared in the pages of *Entertaining*. And I compiled a series of videos on entertaining, with recipes and *tips* that were novel and timely, certainly a result of my busier personal and professional life. ✳ My life has indeed changed since the early eighties. My daughter is grown and living in her own home. I am no longer married, and as a result I entertain a lot more. I have two houses now, and on weekends I like to have lots of houseguests. I cook once or twice during the weekend for large gatherings of *friends* or for small, *intimate* get-togethers. I prefer simpler foods, delicious, of course, but not as rich as I previously prepared. I find I use much less butter and cream in my recipes, many more herbs and spices, and lots of seafood and fruit. I still have a *penchant for desserts*—I cannot fathom entertaining without something *special* as an end to the meal! ✳ I've arranged this book into chapters, each representing my ideas for a specific and special form of entertaining. The pictures display the kinds of table settings, flower arrangements, and *presentation* ideas that I would suggest for these meals. The recipes reflect my belief that we need simplification today, but their simplified approach still allows for a depth of flavorings and careful preparation and presentation. They take advantage of the *wonderful foods* that are readily available nowadays—products such as fresh, crusty French and country breads, mail-order fish and crustaceans, heretofore exotic fruits and vegetables, *unusual* sausages and salsas, and wonderful baked goods. ✳ I care just as much now about how things taste and look as I did years ago, but now I rely even more on *freshness* and *goodness* as the most important ingredients in my cooking. And I still consider entertaining to be one friend treating others to wonderful foods, to beautiful ideas, to *excellent* conversation. Entertaining has been and continues to be for me, and I *hope* for you, a way to share through thought, effort, and caring—much like friendship itself.

All the best,

Martha

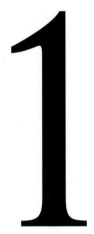

1

Celebrating Spring

Serves 16

Campari and Fresh *Orange* Juice

✳ Fresh *Ham* Baked in Herbs and Cut Green Grass

Smoked Cod *Fish* with Fava Bean Purée

✳ Martha's Mashed *Potatoes*

Sautéed *Cabbage* with a Chiffonade of Basil

Brown Sugar Angel Food Cake with *Blackberry* Sauce

Lemon Angel Food Cake with Butterless Lemon Curd

Celebrating *Spring*

IF I HAD TO CHOOSE ONE ESSENTIAL ELEMENT FOR THE SUCCESS OF AN EASTER

BRUNCH, IT WOULD BE CHILDREN. EVERY EASTER I HAVE AN EGG HUNT IN MY

GARDEN. I INVITE MY NIECES AND NEPHEWS AND AS MANY OF THEIR FRIENDS AS WE

CAN FIND. LAST EASTER MORNING MORE THAN FORTY YOUNG CHILDREN LINED UP

BEHIND THE SILKEN RIBBON IN MY BIG FIELD, WAITING FOR THE RIBBON TO FALL

BEFORE RUSHING OVER HILL AND DALE IN SEARCH OF DOZENS OF BRIGHTLY

COLORED EGGS. DEPENDING ON THE WEATHER (WE EVEN HUNT IN THE SPRING

RAIN), THE CHILDREN DRESS IN EASTER FINERY OR RAINCOATS AND RUBBER BOOTS.

IT IS A HUGE HIT WITH BOTH THE YOUNG AND THEIR PARENTS, THIS ANNUAL CELE-

BRATION, AND AFTER THE HUNT IS OVER I SERVE A GREAT BIG BRUNCH. BECAUSE

OUR FAMILY BACKGROUND IS POLISH, WE ALWAYS HAVE ROASTED SLICED KIELBASA

ON THINLY SLICED RYE BREAD, GARNISHED, OF COURSE, WITH BEET-FLAVORED

HORSERADISH. THERE ARE HARD-BOILED EGGS BY THE DOZEN, TINTED IN PRETTY

PALE COLORS OF BLUE AND GREEN OR LEFT IN THEIR NATURAL HUES IF LAID BY MY

ARAUCANA HENS. I LIKE TO SERVE HAM, EITHER SMOKED OR FRESH, POTATOES IN

SOME FORM OR OTHER, VEGETABLES, SMOKED FISH, FRUIT, AND SOME SPECTACULAR

DESSERTS, ALONG WITH A FEW OF MOTHER'S DELICIOUS BABKAS.

previous page: *I made four angel food cakes for this party, two of each recipe. The lemon-flavored cake was filled with butterless lemon curd and decorated with pansies and violas from the spring garden.*

above: *My niece Sophie celebrates her birthday on April 19, and she considers the Golden Egg her special birthday treat. I always gild and hide at least two, one for Sophie to find (and she always does), and one for someone else to discover. This is a goose egg, very impressive in its little glass flowerpot stand.*

left: *The Easter buffet table was very elaborate this year. I used a long, narrow country table for the display and self-service of food. Because we had so many guests, I used several types of large dinner plates in Easter-egg tones. I covered the table with two heavily crocheted white linen bedspreads. A moss-covered bowl was perfect for the Araucana eggs. I brought out more amber and yellow Depression goblets and pitchers, as well as footed glass pedestals for the cakes. And from the rafters of the white painted pergola, blown-out and colored eggs were hung after being secured, using a hot glue gun, to long "ribbons" of natural raffia.*

CAMPARI *and* *Fresh* ORANGE JUICE

For each 8-ounce glass

The Easter "cocktail" of Campari and fresh orange juice can be made nonalcoholic by using cranberry or pomegranate juice as a substitute for the Campari.

  4 ounces fresh orange juice
  2 ounces soda water
  1 ounce Campari

Mix all of the ingredients and serve in tall glasses over ice cubes.

Fresh HAM *Baked* *in* HERBS *and* CUT GREEN GRASS

Serves 16

The most wonderful way to cook a large haunch of meat is to braise it in the oven and then roast it until golden brown. This ham is tender and tasty, and its roasted herbs and fresh-cut grass add both color and flavor.

  1 18-pound fresh ham
 18 garlic cloves
  1 bunch chervil with flowers
  1 bunch basil
  1 bunch thyme
 10 young, tender bay leaves
      Salt and freshly ground pepper
 ½ pound fresh cut grass, 6–10
      inches long, washed and stored
      in cold water (see Note)
  1 bunch chives
  1 bunch tarragon
  1 bunch parsley
  2 oranges, sliced thick
  1 bottle of dry rosé or dry
      white wine

The fresh ham is placed in a pan lined with fresh-cut green grass, herbs, garlic, and orange slices. I used a large shallow roasting pan and covered it loosely with aluminum foil.

Preheat the oven to 325° F.

With a boning knife, trim all but ¼ inch of fat from the ham, leaving 4 inches of rind around the shank. Using a paring knife, make small incisions in the meat, about ½ inch deep and ¼ inch apart. Peel 10 of the garlic cloves and slice them lengthwise. Insert the garlic slices with alternating sprigs of chervil flowers, basil, thyme, and bay leaves. The herbs and garlic should almost cover the meat. Lightly sprinkle with salt and pepper. Crush the remaining 8 garlic cloves, leaving them in their peels, and set aside.

Line a large round roasting pan 5¾

inches high and 16 inches in diameter with the fresh cut grass, about 1 inch thick on the bottom and around the sides. Reserve some grass and herbs for presentation. Layer the chives, tarragon, and parsley on the bottom and sides of the pan. Place the orange slices on top of the herbs and then cover the orange slices with the basil. Place the ham in the roasting pan with the crushed cloves of garlic and gently pour the entire bottle of wine around the meat. Bake for 30 minutes and then cover loosely with aluminum foil. Continue to braise for another 5 hours, basting if necessary. Remove the foil for the last half-hour of cooking to lightly brown the meat.

When the ham has finished cooking, remove it from the roasting pan to a carving board and allow it to sit, loosely covered with aluminum foil, for 30 minutes before slicing.

While the ham is resting, strain the cooking juices from the roasting pan through a sieve into a saucepan, saving the orange slices. Add them to the juices. Over medium heat, allow the juice to gently boil and reduce by half. Skim off the fat and strain the liquid again to remove the orange slices. Serve hot with the ham on a large platter, garnished with the reserved grass and herbs.

Note: Locate an area in advance with tender, young, organically grown grass that has not yet been cut. It is best to cut it very early in the morning while the dew is still evident; this will prevent the grass from drying out while you are cutting it. Wrap cut grass in damp paper towels to keep it fresh until it reaches the kitchen sink. Wash the grass thoroughly in cold water and keep it in a bowl of cold water until ready to use.

Smoked COD FISH *with* FAVA BEAN *Purée*

Serves 16

A fava bean purée is an excellent accompaniment to the fresh smoked taste of these cod fish fillets. I used a smoker with a combination of charcoal and wood chips to cook the fish.

- 6 tablespoons (¾ stick) unsalted butter
- 2 garlic cloves, chopped
- 3 2-pound fillets of cod fish
- 2 tablespoons extra-virgin olive oil
- ½ teaspoon freshly grated nutmeg
- ½ teaspoon coriander seed, crushed
  Salt (see Note) and freshly ground pepper
  Zest of three oranges
  Fava Bean Purée (recipe follows)
  Sprigs of fresh cilantro, for garnish

Prepare the smoker.

In a small saucepan, melt the butter. Add the garlic and sauté until it is barely soft. Do not allow the butter to brown.

Place the cod fish fillets in a large rectangular glass baking dish. Pour the olive oil and then the garlic butter evenly over the fillets. Sprinkle with the nutmeg, coriander, salt, pepper, and orange zest, and cover the dish with plastic wrap. Allow the fish fillets to marinate for 45 minutes in the refrigerator.

Smoke the fish for 10 to 20 minutes, until it just flakes. Transfer to a serving platter. Garnish with dollops of Fava Bean Purée and cilantro sprigs.

Note: Except for when I prepare pastries, I use coarse kosher salt when I cook. It imparts a better taste and consistency, and enhances natural flavors.

Whenever I start to cook a large meal I go to my herb garden or to my planted pots of herbs and pick a bit of everything. In this way I have learned to enhance my cooking with a number of different flavors and I can also rely a lot less on salt and spices. Always place your cut herbs upright in a big bowl filled with just enough water to wet the stem ends.

Fava Bean Purée

Serves 16

- 6 garlic cloves
- 2 tablespoons extra-virgin olive oil
- 1 pound shelled fresh fava beans
  Salt and freshly ground pepper
- ½ cup water
- 2 tablespoons prepared horseradish
- ½ cup warm milk

Preheat the oven to 400° F. Roast 3 of the garlic cloves by placing them, unpeeled, in a small ceramic baking dish. Drizzle with a little olive oil and bake for 30 minutes, until the garlic is soft and slightly browned. Set aside to cool completely.

While the garlic is roasting, peel and chop the remaining 3 garlic cloves. Shell the fava beans and set aside. Heat the olive oil in a sauté pan and add the chopped garlic with salt and pepper

to taste. Sauté over medium-high heat, being careful not to brown the garlic, as this will change the color of the purée. Add the fava beans to the pan; sauté for 8 to 10 minutes.

Pour in the water, cover the pan with a lid, and simmer for 10 minutes over low heat or until the beans are soft, stirring occasionally.

Slip the beans from their casings, being careful to save as much of the liquid and garlic as possible. Place the beans, the cooking liquid, the roasted garlic, and the horseradish in a food processor and purée until smooth. With the processor running, pour the warm milk through the feed tube and continue to purée until smooth again.

Martha's MASHED POTATOES

Serves 16

These mashed potatoes are rich, it's true, but infinitely edible.

- 2½ pounds Yellow Finn or California long white potatoes, washed and peeled
- ½ cup (1 stick) unsalted butter, cut in pieces
- 1 8-ounce package cream cheese, cut in pieces
- ¼ cup heavy cream
  Salt and freshly ground pepper

Cut the potatoes in quarters, place them in a large stockpot with water to cover, and boil them over high heat uncovered for 30 minutes, or until soft. Drain and mash them with a potato masher, or pass them through a food mill. While hot, add the butter, cream cheese, heavy cream, and salt and pepper to taste. Whip until smooth with a wooden spoon.

Sautéed CABBAGE *with a* CHIFFONADE *of* BASIL
Serves 16

My big platter of sautéed cabbage had to be refilled three times during brunch.

- 1 bunch basil, washed, dried, and stemmed
- 4 tablespoons (½ stick) unsalted butter
- 1 tablespoon extra-virgin olive oil
- 2 pounds green cabbage, finely shredded
- ½ pound bok choy, finely shredded
  Salt and freshly ground pepper

To make a chiffonade of basil leaves, stack 4 to 6 leaves in the same direction. Tightly roll them lengthwise and with a sharp knife, slice thinly to create long, thin strips.

In a sauté pan, melt the butter with the olive oil over medium heat. Combine the cabbage and bok choy and sauté until just soft. Season with salt and pepper to taste.

Stir in the basil chiffonade. Toss until evenly mixed. Serve on a platter side by side with the mashed potatoes.

above: *Fresh cod is usually available at Easter time, and the fillets are delicious smoked with savory spices.*
right: *The blue-edged platter that I used to serve the mashed potatoes and sautéed cabbage is nineteenth-century Leeds, and the silver spoons are nineteenth-century English.*

This is such a beautiful cake. Sitting on its pedestal, in a dark purple purée of blackberry, the Brown Sugar Angel Food Cake attracted lots of attention. I decorated the whipped cream–filled concoction with a Thompson and Morgan pansy called 'The Joker' and plump blackberries.

Brown Sugar ANGEL FOOD CAKE

Serves 10

Made with sifted brown sugar instead of white, angel food cake takes on a very appealing character and taste.

1¼ cups sifted cake flour, non-self-rising
1½ cups light brown sugar, sifted
14 large egg whites, at room temperature
1½ teaspoons cream of tartar
2 teaspoons lemon zest
Whipped Cream Filling (recipe follows)
Whole blackberries
Fresh edible flowers, such as pansies and nasturtiums
Blackberry Sauce (recipe follows)

Preheat the oven to 350° F.

Combine the cake flour with ¾ cup of the sugar. Sift the mixture twice and reserve.

In a large bowl, beat the egg whites with a whisk or an electric mixer at medium speed until foamy. Add the cream of tartar. Increase speed to high and beat the egg whites until thick and tripled in volume. Sprinkle half the remaining sugar over the egg whites and continue beating until the sugar is incorporated. Repeat this step with the remaining sugar and continue beating until the egg whites are stiff and glossy.

Fold in the cake flour and sugar mixture in three additions. With the last addition, add the lemon zest.

Spoon the cake batter into an unbuttered 10-inch angel food cake pan with a removable bottom. Run a knife through the batter to break any air bubbles. Bake for 45 minutes, until the cake is golden in color and springs back when gently pressed with your fingertip.

Invert the pan on a cooling rack and allow the cake to cool completely, at least 1 hour. To remove the cake from the pan, run a knife around the sides and the center tube of the pan. Release the cake from the sides, and run a long knife along the bottom of the cake, freeing it from the tube.

Carefully cut the cake in half horizontally and spread a layer of the whipped cream filling, about 1 cup, on the bottom half of the cake. Arrange whole blackberries in the filling and replace the top half of the cake. Heap the remaining whipped cream on top of the cake and decorate with clean, edible fresh flowers. Serve with the blackberry sauce.

Whipped Cream Filling

Makes 3 cups

1 cup heavy whipping cream
½ teaspoon vanilla extract
2 tablespoons confectioners' sugar

Chill a large metal mixing bowl and your beaters. Using the mixer at high speed, whip the cream with the vanilla and sugar until stiff peaks form.

Blackberry Sauce

Makes 2 cups

3 pints blackberries
1 tablespoon fresh lemon juice
2 tablespoons crème de cassis or blackberry liqueur
5 tablespoons sugar

In a large saucepan combine all the ingredients and cook over low heat, stirring often, until the sugar is dissolved and the sauce begins to thicken, about 20 minutes.

Put through a fine sieve, pressing on the pulp. Discard the seeds.

Lemon ANGEL FOOD CAKE

Serves 10

The tart taste of lemon curd contrasts nicely with the sweet cake.

1¼ cups sifted cake flour, non-self-rising
1½ cups superfine sugar
14 large egg whites, at room temperature
1½ teaspoons cream of tartar
2 tablespoons lemon zest
Butterless Lemon Curd (recipe follows)
Confectioners' sugar, for dusting
Fresh edible flowers, for garnish

Follow the recipe for Brown Sugar Angel Food Cake, substituting superfine sugar for the brown sugar and increasing the amount of zest.

After you cut the cake in half horizontally, hollow out the center of its bottom half. Fill with lemon curd and replace the top half. Dust the cake with confectioners' sugar and decorate with clean, edible fresh flowers.

Butterless Lemon Curd

Makes 2 cups

8 egg yolks
¾ cup superfine sugar
¾ cup plus 2 tablespoons fresh lemon juice
1½ teaspoons grated lemon rind

Whisk the ingredients in a steel or heat-proof glass bowl. Place the bowl over a pan of water that is very lightly simmering, whisking the mixture constantly until it is thick, fluffy, and pale yellow in color. Do not overheat or the yolks will curdle. Allow it to cool completely, about 30 to 35 minutes, before assembling the cake.

Pressed-glass kitchen bowls are used at Easter time to hold the dyes in which to color eggs. I prefer paste vegetable food colorings, boiling water to dissolve the tints and adding a tablespoon or two of distilled white vinegar to help set the colors. I hard-boil quail, chicken, duck, and goose eggs, and color or gild them all for decoration and the hunt.

Our Easter-egg hunt is an essential element of our celebration of spring. Each year I try new colors for the eggs. This year greens and aquas took precedence. It's amazing how many variations on these hues could be concocted.

first: I started making succulent baskets after I discovered Teddy Colbert in Los Angeles. She showed me how to grow succulents and sedums in shapes, rather than in pots. Using soil-filled moss forms over rigid wire, one can plant bowls and wreaths in a variety of sizes and configurations. This time, I planted a living bowl, which worked nicely as a container for Easter eggs.

second: The outside of a wire frame is first covered with a coating of damp sheet moss (green facing out). A layer of rich potting soil is applied to the inside; this in turn is covered with another layer of moss, which is wired into place and secured.

third: Small cuttings of hardened-off sedums are inserted into the moss with tweezers. A pencil point can be used to make holes. Once the shape is covered with enough cuttings, it should be watered every five days for a month until the cuttings take hold. A well-planted bowl or wreath will last for years if properly cared for.

above: *Akro agate flowerpots in pale green doubled as vases for bouquets of spring flowers: lamb's ears, lupines, wood hyacinths, and chive blossoms.* **left:** *My Buff Cochin rooster was very proud to be photographed.* **opposite:** *I always make pretty baskets for the hunt, and fill them with cushions of hay or soft grass.*

Pink **PEONY** *Dinner Party*

Serves 10

Endive and Roasted *Beet* Salad with Rice Wine Vinaigrette

Roasted *Asparagus* ✳ Baked Thatched *Potatoes*

Roasted *Salmon* with Herbed Stuffing

Lemon Granita ✳ Iced Lemon *Mousse Tart*

Lemon *Meringue* Tart in a Macadamia Nut Crust

Pink PEONY *Dinner Party*

THERE ARE CERTAIN TIMES OF THE YEAR WHEN MY GARDEN LOOKS SO BEAUTIFUL THAT I PLAN SPECIAL DINNERS AND PARTIES TO COINCIDE WITH WHAT'S HAPPENING OUTDOORS. FOR INSTANCE, I LIKE TO HAVE A MAY DAY PARTY; MY GUESTS ARE TREATED TO A VIEWING OF THE EARLY SPRING GARDEN, WHEN THE TULIPS, DAFFODILS, FRITILLARIAS, AND A HUNDRED OR SO FRUIT TREES ARE IN FULL BLOOM. IN EARLY JUNE I LIKE TO ENTERTAIN WHEN THE PEONIES ARE BLOOMING. REPLACING THE LATE MAY POPPIES IN BRILLIANCE AND QUANTITY, THIRTY OR SO DIFFERENT VARIETIES OF PEONIES BLOOM EVERYWHERE IN THE GARDEN. THERE ARE SO MANY THAT I AM COMPELLED TO CUT SCORES FOR DISPLAY ALL OVER THE HOUSE. PICKED AS JUST OPENING BUDS AND ARRANGED IN MANY LOW CONTAINERS AND BOWLS, THEY GRADUALLY UNFURL THEIR PETALS OVER A TEN-DAY PERIOD. TO COINCIDE WITH THE PEONY BLOOMING, THIS DINNER MENU MADE USE OF THE EARLIEST VEGETABLES—SMALL BEETS AND FRESH ASPARAGUS—ALONG WITH A DELICIOUS SPRING SALMON. THE TABLE WAS SET SIMPLY AND ELEGANTLY ON THE PORCH SO WE COULD ENJOY THE VIEW OF THE GARDENS RIGHT UNTIL NIGHTFALL. THE PEONIES LASTED SPLENDIFEROUSLY, JUST UNTIL THE ROSES CAME INTO BLOOM. THEN IT WAS TIME FOR A DINNER CELEBRATING THAT MOST WONDERFUL FLOWER.

previous page: *A fancy dinner party no longer requires a "formal" table. I prefer to set one that reflects the mood of the evening, mixing flatware, tableware, and linens. I placed pale pink peonies amid pale yellow goblets on a table covered in finely woven beige linen. The dishes are drabware, creamware, and yellowware Wedgwood. I used pale yellow Depression glass goblets for the dinner wine and mineral water. The flatware is nineteenth-century English silver combined with American pearl-handled knives and forks.* above: *I found this rare yellowware "basket" long ago at a tag sale. Just two pink peonies, a 'Bessie' and a 'Chiffon Parfait', fill it generously.*

above: *The salad course was served on old Wedgwood plates. The embossed ridges and dotted edges are a pretty design for these creamware plates, made some time after the turn of the century.* **opposite, top:** *It is not difficult to store asparagus once they are purchased. Simply cut off the bottom of the stems and stand the asparagus in a half inch of water in the refrigerator. It is best to cook them as soon as possible to take advantage of their freshness. A good rule of thumb: if the asparagus is less than a half-inch thick, it will not need to be pared or peeled. If it is any larger, peel the bottom third of the asparagus stalk with a vegetable parer. The asparagus will cook faster and will be more tender.*

ENDIVE *and Roasted* BEET SALAD *with Rice Wine Vinaigrette*

Serves 10

This salad is lovely when garnished with the flowers and leaves of chervil.

5 whole beets, washed
8-10 Belgian endives
    Rice Wine Vinaigrette
    (recipe follows)
    Fresh chervil with its flowers

Preheat the oven to 350° F.

To roast the beets, cut off all but 1 inch of the greens. Wrap the beets in aluminum foil and place them on a baking sheet. Bake for 1 to 1½ hours, until they are tender when pricked with a fork. Open the foil and allow the beets to cool.

Using gloves (surgical or kitchen), while the beets are still quite hot, slip off the skins. Let the beets cool completely and dice into ½-inch cubes.

Slice the endives on the diagonal ¼ inch thick. Arrange the endives on individual plates and spoon beets over them. Spoon vinaigrette over each salad and garnish with chervil flowers.

Rice Wine Vinaigrette

4 tablespoons rice wine vinegar
1 teaspoon sugar
2 tablespoons Dijon mustard
½ teaspoon chopped fresh chervil
½ cup extra-virgin olive oil
    Salt and freshly ground pepper

In a bowl, combine the vinegar, sugar, mustard, and chervil. Whisk the olive oil into the mixture. Season with salt and pepper to taste.

Roasted ASPARAGUS

Serves 10

By preheating the pan in which the asparagus is roasted, you shorten their cooking time. You can sprinkle them with a bit of balsamic vinegar and salt and pepper.

2½ pounds fresh asparagus, washed and trimmed

Preheat the oven to 500° F.

Heat the roasting pan in the oven before placing the asparagus into it. Roast for 10 to 15 minutes until just tender and slightly brown.

Baked Thatched POTATOES

Serves 10

Because these potatoes are so good, make more than you think necessary.

4 pounds Yellow Finn or California long white potatoes, washed and peeled
¾ cup (1½ sticks) unsalted butter, clarified (page 195)
½ cup fresh thyme, chopped
    Salt and freshly ground pepper

Preheat the oven to 400° F. Using the zigzag blade of a mandoline, slice the potatoes, alternating the direction with every slice by 180 degrees.

Line a large baking sheet with the potatoes, overlapping them and brushing with the clarified butter. Create a second layer if you have enough potatoes. Sprinkle with the thyme, salt, and pepper. Bake for 30 to 45 minutes, until golden brown and crispy.

below: *The peeled potatoes are sliced very thinly on the zigzag blade of a French mandoline, first in one direction and then in the other. The result is a perfect slice, crisscrossed with a "waffle" design. The waffle-cut potatoes are layered with a sprinkling of melted clarified butter, thyme, and salt. Arranged in a shallow metal pan, they bake quickly and crisply.*

first: Choose a whole, cleaned, very fresh salmon, 8 to 10 pounds in weight. Snip off the fins with kitchen shears. Using a fish scaler, scrape the entire surface of the fish, moving the scaler from tail to head. This can be done under gently running cold water, to prevent the scales from flying all over your kitchen. Cut off the head and tail with a sharp knife.

second: Starting from one side of the belly cavity, slip the knife between the flesh and the ribs. Fold back the flesh as you run the knife along the ribs in long, even strokes. Cut up to the backbone, and then cut horizontally along the ribs to the tail. Be careful not to cut through the skin. Repeat on the other side.

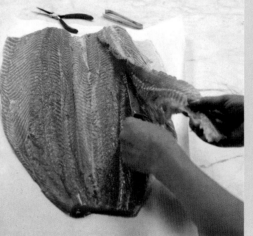

third: With the knife, carefully separate the backbone and ribcage from the flesh, leaving the fish in one flat piece. Use fish tweezers to remove all remaining bones from the flesh. Trim the fatty edges. Everything up to this point can be done several hours before stuffing the fish. Keep it well chilled in the refrigerator.

fourth: Lay the whole boned fish flat, skin side down. Spread the filling evenly over the entire surface of the fish, pressing the layer flat. Fold the fish in half and tie at 1½-inch intervals with cotton kitchen twine, securing the filling down the length of the fish.

fifth: The fish is roasted in a preheated hot oven on a preheated pan. It will cook quite quickly (in about 30 minutes). A good rule of thumb is 10 minutes per inch of thickness. But do not overcook—the fish will get mealy and dry.

sixth: If the skin did not brown in your oven, place the whole fish under a preheated broiler for 1 to 2 minutes to turn the skin golden brown. Let the fish rest out of the heat for 5 minutes before slicing into individual servings. Of course, don't forget to remove the string before serving.

Roasted SALMON *with Herbed* STUFFING

Serves 10

This roasted salmon, filled with a savory stuffing, is as unusual as it is delicious.

3½ ounces bean thread noodles

 2 tablespoons extra-virgin olive oil

 4 medium red onions, cut in half and sliced thinly

 4 garlic cloves, chopped

 5 carrots, peeled and julienned

 2 parsnips, peeled and julienned

 1 medium fennel bulb, julienned

 4 scallions, sliced lengthwise and cut into 2-inch pieces

 1 cup cilantro, chopped
   Salt and freshly ground pepper

 1 10-pound whole salmon, head and tail off, boned

Cook the noodles in a pot of boiling water for 4 to 6 minutes, until tender. Drain and set aside.

Meanwhile, in a large skillet, heat the olive oil over medium-high heat. Sauté the onions for 2 minutes; add the garlic and sauté for 1 minute, then add the carrots, parsnips, fennel, scallions, and cilantro. Sauté the vegetables for 3 to 4 minutes, adding the noodles for the last minute of cooking. Season with salt and pepper. Remove from heat and allow to cool.

Preheat the oven to 500° F. Fill the cavity of the salmon with the stuffing. Using kitchen string, tie the cavity of the salmon closed, tying strings every 1½ inches to secure the stuffing.

Heat a heavy baking sheet in the oven. Line the sheet with parchment paper and place the salmon in it. Roast the salmon for 30 minutes at 500° F., then brown the fish under the broiler for 1 to 2 minutes. Do not burn! Allow the salmon to sit for 5 minutes before cutting into slices. Remove the string before serving.

This is an easy way to cook and serve a whole fish. I was inspired to create this recipe with a "fancy" filling because I loved Eli Zabar's simpler onion-filled version at E.A.T. in New York.

Lemon GRANITA

Serves 10

If the lemons are not to be served in glasses or cups, cut off a bit of their pointed ends so they can stand by themselves on a plate.

3 cups water
1 cup sugar
10 sprigs lemon balm
½ cup fresh lemon juice
2 lemons rinds, finely grated
¼ cup lemon-flavored vodka
10 whole lemons for shells
   Almond extract

In a heavy saucepan, bring the water, sugar, and 5 sprigs of the lemon balm to a boil over medium-high heat until the sugar is dissolved. Discard the lemon balm and cool the syrup over a bowl of ice water until cold.

Whisk together the syrup, lemon juice, lemon rind, and vodka in a metal bowl and place in the freezer. Whisk the mixture every 30 minutes until frozen, about 2 to 3 hours.

Remove any ink on the lemons by rubbing with almond extract. Cut ¼ from the stem end of each lemon. Using a grapefruit knife, cut between the pulp and the pith (white layer between pulp and skin), and remove the pulp with a grapefruit spoon or melon baller, scraping the shell clean.

Using a teaspoon, mound each lemon with granita. Keep in the freezer until ready to serve.

Remove from the freezer, garnish each with half a sprig of lemon balm, and serve immediately.

above: *Lemon Granita is a refreshing and much-appreciated dessert. Search for large, fragrant, bright yellow lemons; Meyer lemons or an extra sour, tart variety will add a unique flavor to the granita. I used some small cordial glasses to serve the lemons. The glasses were discovered, complete with my initial "S," at a local tag sale. I am told they are old Baccarat.* **opposite:** *For dinner parties I often make more than one dessert—it is fun to have a dessert buffet. This buffet looked quite spectacular arranged on a separate table, with the lemons standing on a pale yellow Depression-glass cake stand and the lemon mousse tart presented on a tray of Irish glass. Bright orange poppies, both 'Oriental' and 'Icelandic', were arranged in tiny glasses.*

Iced Lemon MOUSSE TART

Serves 10

The rectangular lemon mousse tart must stay in the refrigerator until right before serving.

1   package unflavored gelatin
1   tablespoon water
½ cup fresh lemon juice
1   cup plus 1 tablespoon sugar
2   lemons rinds, finely grated
5   large egg whites
1   cup crème fraîche (page 40)
2   cups heavy whipping cream
1   rectangular Sugar Crust
     (page 174), prebaked
     Candied Lemon Strips
     (recipe follows)

Dissolve the gelatin in the water in a small saucepan. Add the lemon juice and 1 cup of sugar. Stir over low heat until the gelatin and sugar are thoroughly dissolved. Remove from heat, add the lemon rind, and chill to a syrup consistency. (The gelatin mixture must be cool but not set before being added to the egg whites.)

With an electric mixer or large whisk, beat the egg whites until they are almost stiff. Gradually add the lemon-gelatin mixture and continue to beat the egg whites until they are stiff.

In a separate bowl, whip the crème fraîche until it thickens, then gently fold it into the egg white mixture. Pour the filling into the prepared pie shell and chill in the refrigerator for at least 2 to 3 hours.

When the filling has set, whip the whipping cream in a bowl with the remaining 1 tablespoon of sugar until almost stiff.

To decorate the tart, put the whipped cream in a pastry bag. Use Ateco tip #113 to create a basket-

weave effect and Ateco tip #47 for the bows around the edges. Garnish with candied lemon strips placed on top of the basketweave.

Candied Lemon Strips

2   lemons
2   cups sugar
⅔ cup water

Using a stripper (a tool similar to a zester, but which cuts a wider strip) or a very sharp paring knife, remove the yellow rind from the lemons, trying to leave strips intact.

In a small heavy saucepan, combine the sugar and the water. Bring to a slow rolling boil, and then lower the heat to a simmer. Add the strips of lemon peel and cook for approximately 40 minutes.

Let the mixture cool and then remove the strips. Shape them into small bows and place on wax or parchment paper. Allow them to harden before using to decorate the Iced Lemon Mousse Tart.

Lemon MERINGUE TART *in a* MACADAMIA *Nut Crust*

*Makes one
3½ by 12½-inch tart*

The meringue topping of this tart is not as high as that of my old-fashioned pies, but it is just as delicious. I used Meyer lemons for the filling, which impart a unique sweet-sour flavor to the tart.

1 Macadamia Nut Crust (recipe follows), baked and cooled

Lemon Filling

½ cup cake flour, non-self-rising
1¼ cups sugar
4 large egg yolks
1½ cups water
   Grated rind of 2 lemons
⅓ cup fresh lemon juice

Meringue

3 large egg whites
½ teaspoon cream of tartar
¾ cup superfine sugar (reserve 1 tablespoon for dusting)

To make the filling, in the top of a double boiler whisk together the flour, sugar, egg yolks, water, and lemon rind. Heat the mixture, stirring constantly, over simmering, not boiling, water until thick.

Remove the mixture from the heat and whisk in the lemon juice. Allow the filling to cool for 15 minutes, then transfer it to the cooled macadamia nut crust.

Preheat the oven to 300° F.

To make the meringue, in a large bowl beat the egg whites with a balloon whisk or electric mixer. Add the cream of tartar.

Continue beating the eggs until they are fluffy, then gradually add the sugar, ¼ cup at a time. Beat until the mixture is stiff and glossy.

Heap the meringue on top of the filled tart, and then sprinkle the top of the tart with the reserved tablespoon of sugar.

Bake for 30 minutes or until the meringue is a light brown color. Allow the tart to cool before serving.

Macadamia Nut Crust

*Makes two
3½ by 12½-inch
shells or twelve
3-inch tart shells*

10 ounces finely chopped macadamia nuts
3 cups unbleached all-purpose flour
⅓ cup sugar
1 cup (2 sticks) unsalted butter, cut into small pieces
1 large egg, lightly beaten
1 teaspoon vanilla extract
   Grated rind of 1 lemon

Lightly butter the tart or tartlet pans.

In a food processor, combine the chopped macadamia nuts, flour, and sugar. Add the butter and process until just combined. Add the egg and vanilla. Process until all the ingredients are well mixed.

Divide the mixture and press into the prepared pans. (If making only one tart, freeze the extra dough, well wrapped in plastic.) Chill for at least 30 minutes. Preheat the oven to 350° F. Bake the crust for 20 to 25 minutes, or until the shells are golden brown. Let cool on racks before filling.

opposite: *The lemon meringue tart was baked in an unusual narrow rectangular crust, which made it easy to serve. It worked very well in this menu as part of a dessert sampling, which is what most of the guests wanted.* **left:** *Masses of flowers fresh from the garden were cut short and arranged in low glass bowls.*

3

Hors d'Oeuvres *in the* GARDEN

Serves 40

✳ *Fresh Crab* Dip with Vegetables

Zucchini Rounds with Gorgonzola

Gravlax on Herbed Toast

Oysters en Brochette ✳ *Parmesan* Crackers

Brown *Lentils* and Black Beans on *Cucumber* Rounds

✳ *Tuna* Tartare on Potato Chips

Hors d'Oeuvres

in the GARDEN

I HAVE WORKED ON MY WESTPORT GARDEN FOR MORE THAN TWENTY YEARS, AND ALTHOUGH I STILL CALL IT A "WORK IN PROGRESS," IT IS NOW QUITE PICTURESQUE. VERY OFTEN I ENTERTAIN OUT-OF-DOORS, EITHER UNDER THE PERGOLA AT THE MAIN HOUSE, OR AROUND THE POOL, OR AT THE BIG RED BARN, WHERE THERE IS LOTS OF GOOD GREEN GRASS ON WHICH TO SET UP LAWN FURNITURE. I'VE ACCUMULATED A COLLECTION OF WORKADAY ANTIQUES—GARDEN CARTS, WHEELBARROWS, OLD WIRE COOLING RACKS—THAT COME IN HANDY WHEN SERVING OUTSIDE. THEY CAN'T BE EASILY DAMAGED AND THEY ALWAYS LOOK APPEALING IN THE GARDEN. THE FOOD I SERVE AT GARDEN PARTIES VARIES WITH THE TYPE OF PARTY AND THE TIME OF YEAR; WHAT I SERVE TO DRINK IS BASED ON MY BUDGET, ON THE MENU, AND ON THE PREFERENCES OF MY GUESTS. SOME OF MY FRIENDS WANT ONLY WHITE WINE OR CHAMPAGNE, SOME PREFER MY FRESH MIXED DRINKS, AND OTHERS REALLY JUST WANT ICED TEA OR ICED COFFEE. I HAVE DOZENS OF GLASSES THAT I USE FOR OUTDOOR PARTIES. I THINK THAT ANYONE WHO ENTERTAINS A LOT SHOULD HAVE AN ASSORTMENT OF APPROPRIATE GLASSES STORED IN A CLOSET OR BASEMENT. THESE DON'T HAVE TO BE EXPENSIVE, BUT HAVING THEM ELIMINATES THE NEED TO RENT GLASSES OR THE TEMPTATION TO USE PLASTIC OR PAPER.

previous page: *I used old cooling racks made from decorative wire as hors d'oeuvres trays.* this page: *An old red painted lazy Susan from a country store display is laid with hosta leaves and the curly leaves of variegated flowering kale. These make excellent "trays" for hors d'oeuvres: if the leaves become messy during the party, they can be easily removed or replaced with additional leaves.*

Fresh CRAB DIP *with* VEGETABLES

Serves 40

I garnish the crab dip with sprigs of fresh dill, although chervil, parsley, or cilantro would be delicious, too. As a festive way to serve the crab dip, you can use the top shell portion from a large Dungeness crab. The crab will also provide fresh meat for the dip.

¾ cup mayonnaise
¾ cup crème fraîche (see Note)
1 teaspoon finely grated lemon
   zest
1½ teaspoons Tabasco sauce
½ teaspoon freshly grated nutmeg
½ teaspoon finely minced garlic
   Salt and freshly ground pepper
2 pounds lump crabmeat, picked
   over for cartilage
2 pounds sugar snap peas, stems
   removed
3 red bell peppers, seeded and
   quartered
3 yellow bell peppers, seeded and
   quartered
3 orange bell peppers, seeded and
   quartered
1 bunch dill for garnish

In a large bowl, mix together the mayonnaise, crème fraîche, lemon zest, Tabasco, nutmeg, garlic, salt, and pepper. Gently fold in the crabmeat. Keep covered and in the refrigerator until ready to serve.

Blanch the sugar snap peas in boiling water for 2 minutes. Drain, then immediately plunge them into a bowl of ice water. Drain well. Store them in a plastic bag in the refrigerator until ready to serve. Cut triangular pieces from the quartered peppers. These should also be kept refrigerated in plastic bags until ready to serve. Add a dry paper towel to each plastic bag to absorb excess moisture.

To serve, put a teaspoon of dip on each of half the pepper triangles, garnish with sprigs of fresh dill and arrange on a platter. On a separate platter, arrange the remaining pepper triangles and the peas around a Dungeness crab shell or a decorative bowl filled with dip.

Note: If crème fraîche is not available, combine 2 cups of non-ultrapasteurized heavy cream with 4 tablespoons of buttermilk. Set aside at room temperature for 10 to 24 hours, then refrigerate. Crème fraîche will thicken in 2 days.

ZUCCHINI ROUNDS *with* GORGONZOLA

Serves 40

These can be prepared several hours in advance. Keep refrigerated, then bake at the last minute.

10 small zucchini
½ pound chilled gorgonzola
   cheese, cut into small pieces
2 pints cherry tomatoes, sliced
   thinly
   Baby basil leaves
⅓ pound Parmesan cheese, finely
   grated
   Freshly ground pepper

Preheat the oven to 400° F. Line a baking sheet with parchment paper.

Wash the zucchini and slice them in ½-inch rounds. With a melon baller, scoop out the center of each slice of zucchini, leaving the bottom of each round intact.

Place ½ teaspoon of gorgonzola on each zucchini round. Next, position a slice of cherry tomato on each round; top with a tiny leaf of basil, and sprinkle with Parmesan cheese and pepper.

Place the zucchini rounds on the baking sheet and bake for 5 to 7 minutes. The cheese should be melted but not browned. Garnish with fresh baby basil leaves. Serve immediately.

GRAVLAX

Serves 40

Gravlax is much less oily than smoked salmon. It is delicious on herbed toast with a bit of horseradish dressing.

½ cup coarse salt
½ cup coarsely ground black
   pepper (use a fragrant pepper
   such as Tellicherry or Lampong)
⅓ cup sugar
1 3-pound boned fillet of salmon,
   skin on
1 bunch dill, washed and patted
   dry
   Herbed Toast (recipe follows)
   Horseradish Dressing
   (recipe follows)

In a medium bowl, combine the salt, pepper, and sugar. Cut the salmon fillet in half crosswise. Sprinkle one half with the seasoning mixture to completely cover the surface. Arrange the entire bunch of dill evenly on top of the seasoning. Top with the second fillet and wrap tightly with plastic wrap. Place the fish in a glass or steel baking dish. (The dish must have sides at least ½ inch high in order to retain the juices that will seep from the salmon as it marinates.)

Place a heavy weight on top of the salmon (I use a cast-iron skillet) and put the dish into the refrigerator. Marinate the fillets for 3 days, turning the fish every 12 hours.

To slice, separate the fillets, remove the dill, and scrape off the remaining salt, pepper, and sugar. Cut the salmon into pieces about 2 inches wide. Then slice very thinly with a sharp salmon knife. Serve each piece on herbed toast and top with horseradish dressing.

left: *The crab dip would be great on chips or crackers, or with vegetables. I cut red, yellow, and orange peppers into triangles, prepared some hors d'oeuvres for passing, and let guests dip their own while standing around the table.*

right and below: *Hollowed zucchini rounds filled with tomato and herbs are a favorite light hors d'oeuvre. The finely worked wire rack, blackened with age, is an example of the beautifully crafted kitchen objects that are so collectible.*

left and above: *Although many people love the taste of smoked salmon, gravlax is a fresh-tasting alternative. This well-prepared "pickled" salmon is very nice, especially in the warm-weather months. Use thin baguettes to make the toast.*

right: *On my last trip to Japan I discovered Japanese-style bread crumbs. Resembling shredded coconut, these crumbs adhere well to the oysters, are very light, and cook to a good golden brown color.*

left: *An old wheelbarrow was an excellent solution to the problem of an outdoor bar.* below: *It was May when we had this garden party and the lilacs, giant alliums, and German irises were in full bloom. Massed in a green polka-dotted pitcher, they created a beautiful bouquet.*

right: *I first tasted a version of Parmesan crackers on a trip to California. I added poppy seeds and lemon juice to the basic cracker dough. Chilled, then thinly sliced and baked on parchment paper, the dough cooks without puffing, yet is still wonderfully light.*

Hors d'Oeuvres

Herbed Toast

3 French baguettes, sliced ¼ inch thick on the diagonal
½ cup extra-virgin olive oil
½ cup dill, finely chopped
½ cup chervil, finely chopped

Preheat the oven to 350° F.

Line baking sheets with parchment paper and arrange the bread slices in single layers.

In a medium bowl, mix the olive oil and chopped herbs. Brush each slice with the oil mixture and toast in the oven for 5 to 10 minutes, until crisp and golden, not brown. These can be made early on the day of the party and kept, when cooled, in a tightly covered container.

Horseradish Dressing

2 cups whole-milk yogurt, strained
3 tablespoons prepared horseradish
Salt and freshly ground pepper
Fennel sprigs for garnish

Strain the yogurt by placing it in the center of a large piece of cheesecloth folded in half. Let it hang suspended over a bowl until the water drains out and the yogurt is more solid, about 3 hours. In a medium bowl, mix the yogurt with the horseradish, salt, and pepper. Place a dollop of this topping on each of the gravlax toasts and garnish with a fennel sprig.

OYSTERS *en Brochette*

Serves 40

The oysters must be served immediately after frying. Drain them on paper toweling as they are removed from the oil.

¼ cup Tony's Fish Fry spice mix (see page 68 for ordering information)
¾ cup Japanese bread crumbs (available in Asian food shops)
1 quart fresh oysters
1 pound lean smoked bacon, sliced thinly
2 large eggs, lightly beaten
4 cups vegetable oil (canola or very light olive)
Toothpicks
Cocktail skewers, 4 inches long

In a small bowl, combine the Tony's Fish Fry spice mix and the Japanese bread crumbs.

Wrap each oyster in a piece of smoked bacon just long enough to girdle the oyster. Secure with a toothpick. Dip each bacon-wrapped oyster into the beaten egg and then into the bread crumb mixture.

Heat the oil in a deep, heavy stockpot to 375° F. Deep-fry the breaded oysters in the hot oil for 2 minutes until golden brown. Do not overcook. Remove them with a strainer and allow to cool slightly on a baking sheet.

To serve, remove the toothpick, skewer each oyster with a 4-inch-long wooden cocktail skewer, and arrange them on a platter. Serve while hot.

Parmesan CRACKERS

Makes approximately 4 dozen

These crackers are light, flaky, and very tasty, with a crunch of poppyseed.

4 tablespoons (½ stick) unsalted butter, cut into small pieces
¾ cup unbleached all-purpose flour
1½ cups finely grated Parmesan cheese
¼ teaspoon cayenne pepper
½ teaspoon salt
½ teaspoon coarsely ground black pepper
1 large egg yolk
2 tablespoons ice water
1 teaspoon fresh lemon juice
¼ cup poppy seeds

Preheat the oven to 375° F. Line 4 baking sheets with parchment paper.

Using your fingers or a pastry cutter, incorporate the butter into the flour. Mix in the Parmesan, cayenne pepper, salt, and pepper. Beat together the egg yolk, water, and lemon juice. Add this liquid to the dry mixture and lightly mix, using your fingers. Knead the dough just until it is smooth. Roll it into a long roll 1½ inches in diameter and wrap it in plastic wrap. Refrigerate for 1 hour.

Remove the dough from the refrigerator and slice into ¼-inch-thick crackers. Arrange the crackers on the baking sheets. Sprinkle with poppy seeds. Bake for 10 to 15 minutes until golden brown. Cool on a baking rack. The crackers can be stored in a covered tin, or they can be frozen, wrapped well in plastic.

Hors d'Oeuvres

Brown LENTILS and Black BEANS on CUCUMBER ROUNDS

Serves 40

Well-flavored toppings of black beans or brown lentils make these cucumber hors d'oeuvres appetizing and low in calories. Prepare the toppings a few hours ahead so their flavors can develop.

Brown Lentil Topping

- ½ pound brown lentils, rinsed
- 2 cups water
- 2 garlic cloves, minced
- 1 tablespoon coarse salt
- 2 tablespoons extra-virgin olive oil
- ½ jalapeño pepper, finely minced
  Salt and freshly ground pepper
- 1 small red onion, peeled, halved, and finely sliced

Black Bean Topping

- ½ pound dried black beans, rinsed
- 3 cups water
- 2 tablespoons extra-virgin olive oil
- 2 garlic cloves, minced
- 2 shallots, peeled, finely chopped
  Salt and freshly ground pepper
- ½ yellow pepper, seeded and finely chopped

- ¼ cup chopped cilantro leaves
- 6 large cucumbers

To make the brown lentil topping, in a medium saucepan combine the lentils, water, minced garlic, and 1 tablespoon of salt. Bring the mixture to a boil, reduce the heat to a simmer, and cook uncovered until tender, approximately 20 to 30 minutes.

Drain and transfer to a large mixing bowl. Mix with the olive oil, jalapeño pepper, and salt and pepper to taste. Add the onion and mix.

To make the black bean topping, in a medium saucepan combine the beans and water and bring to a boil. Reduce the heat and simmer uncovered over low heat for 1½ hours, or until the beans are just soft. Drain.

In a sauté pan, heat the olive oil over medium-high heat. Add the beans, garlic, shallots, and salt and pepper to taste. Sauté for 2 minutes, mixing thoroughly.

Remove from the heat and allow the mixture to cool to room temperature. Add the yellow pepper and cilantro and mix well.

When ready to serve, wash and dry the cucumbers. Slice crosswise into ¼-inch rounds, spoon the lentil topping and black bean topping on equal numbers of cucumber rounds, and arrange on serving dishes.

TUNA Tartare on POTATO CHIPS

Serves 40

I used delicate, very fresh tuna, but you can use yellowtail, fluke, or red snapper.

- 5 large baking potatoes, washed and peeled
- 3 cups extra-virgin olive oil
- 1 pound fresh tuna
- 3 tablespoons sesame oil
- 4 tablespoons chives, minced
- 3–4 drops Tabasco sauce
  Salt and freshly ground pepper

To make the potato chips, slice the potatoes thinly, using the straight blade of a French mandoline. Immerse in a bowl of cold water to avoid discoloration.

In a large skillet, heat the oil until very hot but not boiling. Carefully slip one quarter of the potato chips at a time into the hot oil. Cook, stirring, until golden brown, about 3 minutes. Remove from the oil with a strainer. Place the chips on a rack to drain.

To make the tuna tartare, cut off the skin from the tuna and mince the fish very finely. In a large bowl, mix the tuna with the sesame oil, chives, and Tabasco. Season with salt and pepper. Cover with plastic and keep refrigerated until ready to serve.

To serve, place a spoonful of tuna tartare on each chip and arrange on a platter. Serve immediately.

left: *Using cucumbers as the base for hors d'oeuvres is a favorite idea of mine, and a healthy and low-calorie alternative to tortilla chips or crackers.*
opposite: *This tuna tartare is one of my newest hors d'oeuvres. The tuna must be impeccably fresh and the potato chips, cut on a French mandoline, must be crispy and golden brown.*

4

A Small but Special *Baby* SHOWER

Serves 6

Cold Pink *Borscht* ✳ *Salpicon*

Shortbread Cookies

Lemon *Brown Sugar* Cookies

Coconut Ice Cream

A Small but Special *Baby* SHOWER

WHEN CAROLYN KELLY, MY ASSISTANT, TOLD ME SHE WAS PREGNANT, IT CAME AS
NO SURPRISE. ALL OF US IN MY OFFICE HAD FIGURED IT OUT A COUPLE MONTHS
EARLIER WHEN SHE STOPPED DRINKING COFFEE AND TEA, A SURE SIGN THESE DAYS.
AS THE MONTHS WENT BY, WE ALL WANTED TO GIVE CAROLYN A SHOWER, AND
FINALLY, TWO WEEKS BEFORE EMILY ANNE WAS BORN, WE HAD A DELIGHTFUL
LUNCH AT MY HOUSE. CAROLYN ALREADY HAD ONE CHILD, GREGORY, AND SHE HAD
HAD SEVERAL SHOWERS DURING HER FIRST PREGNANCY. SHE REALLY WANTED THIS
PARTY TO BE SMALL AND SIMPLE, AND WE KEPT THE MENU SMALL AS WELL. I MADE
THE COLD PINK BORSCHT; NECY CREATED CAROLYN'S FAVORITE SALAD, THE
BRAZILIAN CONCOCTION CALLED SALPICON; AND KATHY AND I COLLABORATED ON
THE DESSERTS—ICE CREAM AND COOKIES. THE DECORATIONS WERE ALSO SIMPLE
BUT CUTE, AND THE COLOR SCHEME WAS PINK, BLUE, AND GREEN. I MADE MIXED
FLOWER ARRANGEMENTS IN ETCHED MERCURY GLASS VASES WITH SPRAY ROSES,
LAVENDER, AND CALADIUM LEAVES, A NEW FAVORITE FOR CUTTING. PALE BLUE AND
AQUA LURAY PLATES COMPLEMENTED THE FOOD. BECAUSE THERE WAS NO "THEME"
TO THIS SHOWER, THE GIFTS RAN THE GAMUT FROM TOYS TO CLOTHES TO ELEGANT
ENGRAVED CALLING CARDS FOR EMILY ANNE KELLY.

previous page: *Two kinds of cut-out cookies were baked, and then decorated in pink, white, and blue with simple patterns.* left: *Carolyn always looked good during her pregnancy, but in the last two weeks even more so.* right: *Ribbon-tied pacifiers were just a lighthearted way of continuing the baby theme.*

above: *Carolyn loves beets, so I cooked a bright pink borscht for her to enjoy. It was garnished with sprigs of fresh dill. The dishes are Luray, pale blue and pale aqua.* right: *The shower was attended by a small gathering of Carolyn's Westport and New Canaan friends.* above right: *All of Carolyn's presents were beautifully wrapped in pale-colored tissues and assorted ribbons.*

left: *I first tasted salpicon years ago at a wedding that Necy catered. It was superb. I have served it many times since and consider it to be a perfect luncheon salad.* right: *Before serving, gently toss the ingredients, including the potatoes, with your hands. No spoon can do as thorough a job without crushing the ingredients.* below: *Because salpicon is a one-dish salad, large helpings are appropriate.*

Cold Pink BORSCHT

Serves 6 to 8

Flavored with dill and served cold, this borscht is a delightful first course.

12 medium beets
1 tablespoon unsalted butter
2 medium yellow onions, peeled and minced
2 carrots, peeled and finely grated
2 teaspoons sugar
6 cups chicken or beef broth
3 tablespoons fresh lemon juice
  Salt and freshly ground pepper
2 cups sour cream, or 1 cup sour cream and 1 cup yogurt
  Fresh dill sprigs for garnish

Preheat the oven to 350° F.

Wash the unpeeled beets. Wrap them in aluminum foil and place them on a baking sheet in the oven. Bake them until fork-tender, about 1 hour. Allow the beets to cool, then slip off the skins and grate them coarsely.

In a large stockpot, melt the butter and sauté the onions and carrots over medium heat for 10 minutes. Add the beets, sugar, and broth and bring to a boil, then reduce the heat. Simmer for 20 to 30 minutes, until the vegetables are tender, then remove from heat. Purée the mixture in a food processor or food mill. Transfer the purée to a large bowl; stir in the lemon juice and season with salt and pepper. Chill in the refrigerator for 30 minutes.

When ready to serve, gently whisk the sour cream into the soup and garnish each serving with sprigs of dill.

SALPICON

Serves 6

This salad must be mixed and tossed together just before serving in order to keep the potatoes crisp. As with every salad, the secret to the success of this one is fresh ingredients.

2 medium onions
2 tablespoons extra-virgin olive oil
3 whole chicken breasts
3 garlic cloves, minced
1 teaspoon coarse salt
1 teaspoon freshly ground pepper
1 tablespoon sweet paprika
⅓ cup parsley, roughly chopped
3 scallions, chopped, white and green parts
1 pound green beans, trimmed
2 pounds carrots
5 pounds white potatoes
  Vegetable oil
½ cup mayonnaise

Peel and mince one of the onions and set aside. In a large, heavy pot, heat the olive oil. Add the chicken breasts to the oil and brown them on both sides for 10 minutes over medium heat. Add the garlic and sauté for 1 minute, then stir in the salt, pepper, minced onion, and paprika. Sauté for 3 to 4 minutes, or until the onion is soft. Pour in 3 cups of water, bring to a boil, then reduce the heat to medium-low and simmer, covered, for 30 minutes.

Add the parsley and scallions; allow them to cook for 5 minutes until softened.

Remove the chicken breasts and place them in a large bowl to cool. Strain the cooking liquid and pour over the chicken to keep it moist.

When the chicken has cooled enough to handle, remove the meat from the bone; discard the skin and bones. Using your fingers, shred the meat, then replace it in the bowl with the cooking liquid. Cover with plastic wrap, and chill in the refrigerator for 30 minutes.

Cut the green beans into ¼-inch pieces and reserve them, covered and chilled, in a separate bowl until ready to use. Wash, peel, and grate the carrots. Reserve them, covered and chilled, in a separate bowl until ready to use. Slice the remaining onion into thin rings. Reserve, covered and chilled, in a separate bowl until ready to serve.

Wash and peel the potatoes, placing them whole in a large bowl of cold water to prevent discoloring.

In a medium stockpot, heat 2 inches of vegetable oil to 375° F. One at a time, grate the potatoes onto a towel, pat dry, and immediately place into the hot oil. Fry until golden brown, then remove them from the oil with a slotted spoon to a large paper-towel-covered surface to drain. Repeat the process until all the potatoes are cooked. Use additional vegetable oil if necessary.

Toss the chicken, potatoes, vegetables, and mayonnaise together in a large serving bowl. Season the salad with salt and pepper and serve immediately.

Shortbread COOKIES

Makes 4 dozen

When baked, these cookies should be very pale in color.

1½ cups (3 sticks) unsalted butter, softened
¾ cup sugar
1 teaspoon vanilla extract
2 cups unbleached all-purpose flour
1 cup cornstarch
Simple Cookie Icing (recipe follows)

Cream together the butter and sugar in a large bowl. Stir in the vanilla.

Sift together the flour and cornstarch. Stir thoroughly into the creamed mixture. Place the dough on a sheet of plastic wrap and form the dough into a flat disc. Wrap the dough and chill it for at least 2 hours.

Preheat the oven to 325° F. Line baking sheets with parchment paper. Roll out the dough on a lightly floured surface and cut out shapes with a cookie cutter. Bake for 5 to 8 minutes. Remove from the baking sheets and cool on racks. Spread on the icing.

Lemon BROWN SUGAR COOKIES

Makes 4 dozen

Use simple cookie cutters for these, or make your own stencils from cardboard.

2½ cups unbleached all-purpose flour
2 teaspoons baking powder
¾ cup (1½ sticks) unsalted butter, softened
½ cup brown sugar
1 teaspoon lemon zest

2 large eggs
Simple Cookie Icing (recipe follows)

Sift together the flour and baking powder.

Cream together the butter, sugar, and lemon zest in a large bowl. Beat in the eggs, then stir in the flour mixture thoroughly. Place the dough on a sheet of plastic wrap and form the dough into a disc. Wrap the dough and chill it for at least 2 hours.

Preheat the oven to 325° F. Line baking sheets with parchment paper. Roll out the dough on a lightly floured surface and cut out shapes with a cookie cutter. Bake for 5 to 8 minutes, until pale golden. Remove from the baking sheets and cool on racks. Spread on the icing.

Simple Cookie Icing

Makes enough for 4 dozen cookies

3½ cups confectioners' sugar, sifted
3 large egg whites, lightly beaten
½ teaspoon fresh lemon juice

Dyes

Sky Blue #1140
Rose Pink #1150
Seafoam Green #1128
Baker's Rose #1151
Leaf Green #1131

In a medium bowl, combine the confectioners' sugar, egg whites, and lemon juice. Blend until smooth.

Divide the icing into small bowls and tint each with Ateco paste dyes. (Liquid dyes work well also.) Blend the colors thoroughly. Apply to cookies immediately. Make in small batches as necessary.

Coconut Ice CREAM

Makes 2 pints

Keep the ice cream in a shallow Pyrex dish in the freezer, covered with plastic wrap touching the surface of the ice cream. This will prevent freezer burn.

1½ cups milk
1½ cups heavy cream
1 cup canned unsweetened coconut milk
8 large egg yolks
½ cup sugar
6 tablespoons cream of coconut
1 teaspoon vanilla extract
2 tablespoons golden rum, such as Mount Gay

In a medium saucepan, combine the milk, cream, and coconut milk. Bring to a boil over medium-high heat, remove from heat, and let sit for 1 hour to blend. Return the saucepan to medium-low heat and bring the mixture to a simmer.

In a mixing bowl, whisk the egg yolks with the sugar until light, fluffy, and pale yellow in color. Slowly add the warm milk mixture while constantly whisking the egg yolks and sugar. Add the cream of coconut and vanilla. Pour this mixture back into the saucepan and heat over low heat for about 15 minutes, constantly stirring until the mixture coats the back of a spoon.

Remove the mixture from the heat and whisk over a bowl of ice until it cools to room temperature. Add the rum and stir well. Using an ice cream machine, follow the manufacturer's directions to make ice cream.

Set upon silver plates, these ice cream goblets, with their bright turquoise bulbous stems, went well with the rest of the green, blue, and pink color scheme. Homemade coconut ice cream was eaten with German ice cream spoons.

5

SPICY **Thai** *Lunch*

Serves 6

Thai Salad ✳ Flavorful *Noodle Soup*

Stuffed Grilled *Shrimp*

Grilled Soft-Shell *Crabs*

Curried *Fruit* Salad

SPICY Thai *Lunch*

MY INTRODUCTION TO THE CUISINES OF SOUTHEAST ASIA HAS BEEN GRADUAL, AND MY EATING EXPERIENCES HAVE BEEN RATHER SPORADIC. NEVERTHELESS, I FIND THAI FOOD TO BE INTRIGUING—IT IS INTENSE AS WELL AS DELICATE, AND SUPERBLY COLORFUL. THE FLAVORS ARE DIVERSE AND LAYERED, SPICY AND SWEET, HOT AND MILD, PUNGENT AND CRISP. THAT IS WHY THE SAME RECIPE WILL HAVE SUCH VARIED INGREDIENTS AS RED PEPPER FLAKES AND BROWN SUGAR, GARLIC AND MINT, GINGER AND CUCUMBER. A BASIC COURSE IN THE COOKING OF THAI FOOD WOULD CERTAINLY INCLUDE A SPICY NOODLE SOUP LIKE THE ONE IN THIS MENU. AND IT WOULD PROBABLY ALSO INCLUDE THE SALAD AND A GRILLED DISH LIKE THE SHRIMP. THIS KIND OF MEAL IS BEST SERVED "FAMILY STYLE," WITH EACH DISH IN ONE LARGE BOWL OR PLATTER, AND THE CONDIMENTS IN MANY SMALL BOWLS. WE ATE OUR THAI LUNCH OUTSIDE, ON THE TERRACE NEAR MY SWIMMING POOL. EVERYTHING THERE—THE POOL, THE PAVING STONE, THE FURNITURE, AND THE CUSHIONS—IS A HUE OF TEAL BLUE-GREEN, SO I USED A BRIGHT TEAL TABLECLOTH, TURQUOISE HOBNAIL GOBLETS, AND WHITE POTTERY DISHES. A CHARCOAL GRILL, LOCATED NOT FAR FROM THE SCENE, WAS CONVENIENT FOR GRILLING THE SHRIMP AND THE SUPERB SOFT-SHELL CRABS.

above: *Picked from my summer garden, these colorful flowers created quite a stir among the guests, some of whom had never seen such large peonies or such gigantic 'Oriental' poppies. I arranged the flowers very simply in an old flower market metal holder.* left: *The soup starts with a clear, unflavored chicken broth. To make it, use a fresh chicken that has not been frozen so that the broth is of the best flavor. The Thai sauce is added to the broth directly before serving, resulting in the layered flavors for which Thai cuisine is renowned. I used a large shallow bowl for the soup.* below: *The grilled shrimp stuffed with fresh pineapple and red chili peppers cook quickly over charcoal. Everyone loved the unique flavor.*

Thai SALAD

S e r v e s   6

Use a simple, large platter like a palette to serve this colorful salad.

S a l a d

2 small heads red leaf lettuce
2 pounds curly leaf spinach
1 small head cabbage, green or purple
1 pound sugar snap peas or snow peas, stem ends trimmed
1 pound green beans, stems removed and sliced on the diagonal
1 pound carrots, peeled and sliced ¼ inch thick on the diagonal
12 scallions, cut in half lengthwise
2 oranges, peeled and sectioned
2 bananas, sliced on the diagonal

D r e s s i n g

6 tablespoons sesame oil
3 teaspoons hot sesame oil
12 tablespoons rice vinegar
3 teaspoons curry powder
3 teaspoons teriyaki sauce
3 teaspoons sugar
½ small chili pepper, seeded and minced
Salt and freshly ground pepper

T o p p i n g s

¼ cup unsalted peanuts
¼ cup dark raisins
1 teaspoon chopped chives, with flowers for decoration (optional)
½ cup mung bean sprouts
½ cup alfalfa sprouts
¼ cup black sesame seeds
¼ cup white sesame seeds

Wash and spin dry the lettuce leaves. Wash the spinach well, then spin dry and discard the stems. Shred the cabbage with a knife. Keep the lettuce, spinach, and cabbage in separate bowls, covered and refrigerated.

Blanch the sugar snap peas or snow peas in boiling water for 1 minute. Drain, then plunge them into a bowl of ice water. Drain again and set aside. Blanch the green beans similarly.

In a medium bowl whisk together the sesame oil, hot sesame oil, rice vinegar, curry powder, teriyaki sauce, sugar, chili pepper, and salt and pepper. Reserve until ready to serve.

On a large serving platter, arrange the red leaf lettuce around the edge and fill the center of the platter with spinach. Arrange the cabbage, beans, peas, carrots, scallions, oranges, and bananas in sections on top of the lettuce and spinach. Sprinkle the toppings over the salad, then pour the dressing over it. Serve immediately.

F l a v o r f u l NOODLE SOUP

S e r v e s   6

This soup offers an extraordinary variety of flavors and textures. It can be served warm or at room temperature.

1 4-pound whole fresh broiler chicken
1 cup nuoc mam fish sauce (available in Asian markets)
3 garlic cloves, peeled and crushed
2 tablespoons chopped fresh ginger, peeled and finely minced
3 tablespoons fresh lime juice
2 tablespoons dark brown sugar
1 teaspoon red pepper flakes
¼ cup water
1 pound cellophane noodles
1 small red onion, halved and sliced
1 bunch scallions, trimmed and cut in 4-inch lengths

C o n d i m e n t s

24 fresh mint leaves
24 fresh cilantro leaves
2 cups mung bean sprouts
1 long cucumber, peeled and sliced ¼ inch thick on the diagonal
2 limes, cut into 8 wedges each
2 orange or red bell peppers, seeded and thinly sliced lengthwise

Place the chicken in a large pot with enough cold water to cover it. Bring the water to a boil and immediately reduce the heat to low, simmering the chicken for 30 to 45 minutes. Remove the chicken and discard the skin and bones. Cut the meat into large pieces and return it to the stock. Allow it to sit covered until ready to serve.

While the chicken is cooking, whisk together in a medium bowl the nuoc mam, crushed garlic, ginger, lime juice, brown sugar, red pepper flakes, and water. Keep the sauce covered with plastic wrap in the refrigerator until ready to serve.

Prepare the condiments and place each vegetable in its own bowl. Cover the vegetables with plastic wrap and keep in the refrigerator until ready to serve.

Right before serving, soak the noodles in warm water for 15 minutes and drain well. Lay the noodles in the bottom of a large serving bowl, arrange the chicken meat on top, then add the sliced onion and scallions. Stir the sauce into the simmering chicken broth and ladle the mixture over the chicken and noodles. Serve the soup immediately with the condiments, allowing guests to add as they like.

The Thai salad was arranged on a large white platter. The ingredients are not complicated—cabbage, scallions, carrots, and green beans, to name a few—but the mixture of fruit and vegetables, combined with a spicy sweet dressing and numerous toppings, makes the salad extremely interesting and very mouthwatering!

Stuffed Grilled
SHRIMP

Serves 6

Leave the shrimp unpeeled to keep the meat very tender during grilling.

18 jumbo shrimp, heads and tails intact
½ cup crushed pineapple, preferably fresh
½ cup seeded and finely diced green bell pepper
1 scallion, sliced thin
¼ teaspoon chili powder
¼ teaspoon coarse salt
Pinch freshly ground pepper

Prepare a charcoal grill and light 1 hour before grilling, or preheat the broiler to high (500° F.).

Using a paring knife, remove legs from the shrimp. Split the shrimp lengthwise down the middle of the underside. Rinse well under cold running water. Dry on paper towels.

In a medium bowl, combine the pineapple, green pepper, scallion, chili powder, salt, and pepper.

Fill each shrimp with 1 tablespoon of the stuffing and cook them on the grill or broil for 3 minutes per side, until pale pink. Serve immediately.

Grilled
SOFT-SHELL
CRABS

Serves 6

After marinating in a spicy blend of flavors, these crabs are delicious grilled quickly over the hot coals.

2 tablespoons sesame oil
¼ cup extra-virgin olive oil
⅓ cup fresh lime juice
1 dash tamari

The bright turquoise hobnail goblets from the thirties were exactly right for this table setting. I served both Chinese beer and Thai beer and made sure they came to the table ice cold.

2 tablespoons ground cumin
2 garlic cloves, minced
2 tablespoons chopped fresh ginger
1 hot pepper, seeded and minced
12 soft-shell crabs, cleaned

In a medium bowl, whisk together the sesame oil, olive oil, lime juice, tamari, and cumin. Stir in the garlic, ginger, and hot pepper.

Place the soft-shell crabs in a glass baking dish, preferably in one layer so they will absorb the marinade evenly. Pour the marinade over the crabs, inserting some of the marinade solids under the shells. Cover the baking dish tightly with plastic wrap and refrigerate for 6 hours.

Prepare a charcoal grill and light 1 hour before cooking, or preheat broiler to high (500° F.).

Discard the marinade and cook the soft-shell crabs on the charcoal grill or in the broiler for 4 to 5 minutes per side, or until they turn reddish. Serve the crabs with the stuffed grilled shrimp.

Curried
FRUIT SALAD

Serves 6

This is a delightful variation on a classic fruit salad. To check for ripeness, smell the melon and the pineapple; they should be wonderfully sweet.

Salad

1 small honeydew melon
1 fresh pineapple
½ orange bell pepper, seeded and diced

Dressing

⅓ cup fresh orange juice
1 teaspoon honey
1 teaspoon grainy mustard
½ teaspoon prepared horseradish
¼ teaspoon curry powder
Salt and freshly ground pepper

Cut the honeydew melon in half and remove the seeds. Slice into eighths and cut off the rind. Cut the melon into small, bite-size chunks. Using a stainless steel knife, remove the top and bottom of the pineapple, then stand it upright and cut away the outer rind. Cut the pineapple into quarters from top to bottom, and remove the core. Cut the pineapple into small, bite-size chunks.

In a serving bowl, toss the fruit and orange pepper together. Keep covered and chilled until ready to serve.

In a small bowl, whisk together the orange juice, honey, mustard, horseradish, curry powder, and salt and pepper to taste. When ready to serve, pour the dressing over the fruit and toss well.

clockwise from top left: *In lieu of small bowls I used porcelain egg cups, opaline finger bowls, and custard cups for the numerous garnishes. The soft-shell crabs should be cleaned right before marinating; I like to tuck some of the marinade solids under the shell to intensify the flavor of the crab. In keeping with the layering of flavors, even the dessert is both sweet and spicy: fresh pineapple, honeydew, and orange sweet pepper are flavored with a sweet dressing that also contains horseradish and curry. The platter of grilled shrimp and crab empties as quickly as the bowl of soup; it is a good idea to grill a few at a time so that the seafood can be served hot to everyone.*

Louisiana *Seafood* FEAST

Serves 18

Tomato, Basil, and *Red Onion* Salad

✳ *Cayenne* Corn Bread

Sweet Onion and *Arugula* Sandwiches

Louisiana-Style *Shrimp*

Seafood Boudin ✳ Spicy *Crawfish*

✳ Lemon Coconut *Buttermilk* Pie

Thelma's *Coconut* Cake

Banana Ginger Custard Delight

Louisiana *Seafood* FEAST

I MET DERO AND BEN PUCKETT AND THEIR LARGE FAMILY IN JACKSON, MISSISSIPPI, IN 1983 DURING MY BOOK TOUR FOR *ENTERTAINING*. AFTER MANY VISITS TO THEIR PART OF THE COUNTRY, I HAVE REALLY LEARNED WHAT SOUTHERN HOSPITALITY IS ALL ABOUT. ALL THE PUCKETTS ARE WARM AND FRIENDLY, BUT THE PARENTS, DERO AND BEN, ARE EXTRAORDINARY. THEY'RE ALWAYS GRACIOUS, ALWAYS GENEROUS WITH INFORMATION, AND ALWAYS AMAZINGLY HOSPITABLE, TREATING ME TO WONDERFUL FEASTS OF LOCAL CUISINE: CRAWFISH AND SHRIMP, GUMBO, CRABS, AND FRESH-CAUGHT FISH. IF A FOOD IS IN SEASON (OR EVEN IF IT ISN'T), DERO CAN LOCATE IT. AND BEN WILL COOK HIS SHRIMP BOILS, SPICY CRAWFISH, AND OYSTER STEWS IN HUGE KETTLES OVER THE BIG OUTDOOR GAS BURNER THAT HE BUILT. IT WAS DERO WHO INSPIRED ME TO CREATE THIS MENU. EXCEPT FOR THE CORN BREAD, SALAD, SANDWICHES, AND DESSERTS, THE FOOD FOR THIS DELICIOUS MEAL WAS ORDERED BY MAIL. THERE ARE MANY SUPPLIERS SUCH AS TONY'S LIVE CATFISH AND SEAFOOD IN BATON ROUGE WHO WILL GLADLY SHIP OVERNIGHT ALL KINDS OF FOOD THAT MAKE ENTERTAINING IN THIS STYLE EASY. TODAY, IT'S POSSIBLE TO EAT SEAFOOD BOUDIN ONE DAY, MEMPHIS BARBECUE THE NEXT, AND TEXAS TAMALES THE THIRD NIGHT—ALL WITHOUT EVER LEAVING HOME.

previous page: *Thelma's Coconut Cake is a nice crumbly yellow cake, filled with crushed pineapple and frosted with a seven-minute–type icing and freshly grated coconut. Three layers make the cake especially impressive.* right: *Homegrown tomatoes are usually best. I try to grow a deep red type of slicing tomato every year for salads and sandwiches.*

above: *Here is the kitchen table, right before the guests sit down. All of the seafood and the boudin are piled separately on huge platters or copper pans. The salad plates at each place setting are for the shrimp peels and crawfish shells. The uncovered table is easy to clean up after the guests have had their go at the abundant food.*

clockwise from top left: *This salad, made when local tomatoes are available, is best composed at the last minute; I look for large, sweet onions (Vidalias, if I can locate them) and lots of fine-leaved fresh basil. Shrimp, highly seasoned with Cajun spices, lemons, and onions, are boiled in the shell for peeling hot at the table; if you can get them, fresh shrimp are the best, but quick-frozen shrimp, defrosted and boiled immediately, are also very good. Whole-wheat soft rolls are my favorite for grilled onion sandwiches; you can also use fresh hamburger rolls or hard rolls for this delicious alternative to the ubiquitous hamburger. I have discovered that Southerners often use sugar in their savory baking and in their vegetable recipes; this corn bread is no exception.*

Louisiana *Seafood* FEAST

Tomato, Basil, and Red Onion SALAD

Serves 18

Red onions are an excellent choice for this salad.

- 5 large ripe red tomatoes
- 2 large red onions, peeled
- ⅓ cup balsamic vinegar
- ¼ cup extra-virgin olive oil
  Salt and freshly ground pepper
- 20 sprigs fresh basilico fino, or 20 large basil leaves

Slice the tomatoes ½ inch thick; slice the onions thinly. Arrange alternating slices of tomatoes and onions on a serving platter. Drizzle the balsamic vinegar and olive oil over the salad. Sprinkle the salad with salt and pepper to taste and garnish with the basil.

Cayenne Corn BREAD

Serves 18

In combination with the cayenne pepper, sugar gives a good flavor to this corn bread.

- 3 cups yellow cornmeal
- 4 cups unbleached all-purpose flour, sifted
- 1 cup sugar
- 4 tablespoons baking powder
- 2 teaspoons salt
- ½ teaspoon cayenne pepper
- 8 large eggs
- 4 cups milk

Preheat the oven to 350° F. Butter two glass 13 by 9-inch baking dishes.

In a large mixing bowl combine the cornmeal, flour, sugar, baking powder, salt, and cayenne pepper. Sift through a coarse sieve. In a separate large bowl lightly beat the eggs and milk. Add the dry ingredients, stirring to combine. Do not overmix.

Pour the batter into the buttered baking dishes and bake for 30 minutes or until a cake tester comes out clean when inserted in the center. Cool and cut into squares.

Sweet Onion and Arugula SANDWICHES

Makes 9 large sandwiches

Cut these tasty sandwiches in half and serve them while the seafood is cooking.

- ½ cup extra-virgin olive oil
- ½ teaspoon coarse salt, plus more for sprinkling
- ½ teaspoon freshly ground pepper, plus more for sprinkling
- 3 large sprigs fresh rosemary
- 3 large sprigs fresh thyme
- 3 large Vidalia onions, peeled and sliced ½ inch thick
- ½ cup mayonnaise
- 9 large whole-grain buns or hard Kaiser buns, split
- 2 bunches arugula, washed and dried

Prepare a charcoal grill and light 1 hour before grilling, or preheat the broiler to 500° F.

In a small bowl, mix the olive oil, salt, pepper, rosemary, and thyme. Place the onion slices in a glass baking dish and evenly pour the marinade over them. Cover the baking dish with plastic wrap and allow the onions to marinate for 45 minutes, turning once to coat evenly.

Grill the onion slices 6 to 8 minutes over medium coals or in the broiler, until they are just tender and slightly blackened.

Assemble the sandwiches by spreading mayonnaise on both sides of each bun. On the bottom of each bun, layer the arugula and then a slice or two of onion. Sprinkle with salt and pepper and top with the second half of the bun. Cut in half and serve.

Louisiana-Style SHRIMP

Serves 18

Make sure the shrimp don't curl tightly, or they will be overcooked.

- 10–12 tablespoons Cajun spice mix
- 1 lemon, sliced
- 4 large onions, sliced
- 10 pounds medium whole shrimp with heads, rinsed

Fill a large stockpot ¾ full with cold water and add the spice mix, lemon, and onion slices. Bring the water to a rapid boil over high heat.

Using a pair of tongs, slide the shrimp into the stockpot. Adjust heat so the water is reduced to a simmer. Gently stir the shrimp with a wooden spoon to make sure they all cook evenly. Allow the shrimp to cook for about 10 minutes, until their shells are pink and their flesh opaque.

Remove the shrimp from the pot with a slotted spoon or Chinese strainer. Serve hot.

SEAFOOD BOUDIN *and Spicy* CRAWFISH

I purchased the fresh seafood boudin (sausage), made from crab, shrimp, and rice, as well as the spicy cooked crawfish from Tony's Live Catfish and Seafood, of Baton Rouge. Places like Tony's enable me to create regional cooking right in my own home. There are now many establishments that will mail their products overnight, cooled with dry ice or ice packs.

To cook the boudin, prick the casing of the sausages with the point of a sharp knife. Place the boudin in a shallow pan, add about ⅓ inch of water, and bring to a simmer. Cook, covered, for 15 minutes, then uncover and cook until all the moisture evaporates. Turn the boudin once or twice during cooking. Serve hot.

Even though I bought my spicy crawfish already cooked, it is not difficult to steam them at home. Layer washed crawfish with spicy crab boil mix, or a homemade mix of spices, in the steamer portion of a very large lobster steamer. Boil about four inches of water in the bottom portion and place the crawfish over the boiling liquid. Allow to steam for about 12 minutes until the crawfish have turned bright red. Cool slightly before eating.

Crawfish can be cooked the day before and eaten cold. There is an art to eating a spicy boiled crawfish. You break off the tail and crack the claws, then extract the meat, using a lobster fork or your fingers.

Order boudin, crawfish, shrimp, and spice mixes from:
Tony's Live Catfish and Seafood
5215 Plank Road
Baton Rouge, Louisiana 70805
504-357-9669

Order wooden mallets and spice mixes for boiling crabs and shrimp from:
Obrycki's Crab House
1727 East Pratt Street
Baltimore, Maryland 21231
800-742-1741
410-732-6399

Lemon Coconut BUTTERMILK PIE

Serves 8

The top of this pie turns an incredible rich golden brown color during baking.

½ cup (1 stick) unsalted butter, at room temperature
2 cups sugar
4 large eggs
⅔ cup buttermilk
1 teaspoon vanilla extract
2 tablespoons fresh lemon juice
2 teaspoons fresh lemon zest
1 cup plus 4 tablespoons shredded coconut (see following recipe)
1 Sugar Crust (page 174), prebaked for 15 minutes in a 10-inch round tart pan with removable bottom

Preheat the oven to 400° F.

In the bowl of an electric mixer, cream the butter and sugar until light and fluffy. Add the eggs one at a time to the butter mixture, beating until pale yellow and creamy. Add the buttermilk, vanilla, and lemon juice, beating until well combined. Add the lemon zest.

Stir in 1 cup of the shredded coconut and pour into the prebaked pie shell. Sprinkle the top of the pie with the remaining coconut and bake for 10 minutes. Reduce the heat to 350° F. and continue baking for an additional 35 to 40 minutes, until the pie is golden brown and the custard is set. Allow the pie to cool on a baking rack before serving.

Thelma's COCONUT CAKE

Serves 12

This dessert gets even better after a day. Refrigerate it if you don't have a cool dark spot in your kitchen.

1 cup (2 sticks) unsalted butter, at room temperature
½ cup vegetable shortening
2 cups sugar
5 large eggs
2 teaspoons vanilla extract
1 cup milk
3 cups unbleached all-purpose flour
2 teaspoons baking powder
2 cups crushed fresh pineapple
1 fresh coconut

Icing

1 cup water
3 cups sugar
3 large egg whites
1 teaspoon vanilla extract

Preheat the oven to 350° F. Butter and flour three 9-inch round cake pans.

Using an electric mixer, cream the butter, shortening, and sugar until light and fluffy.

Add the eggs one at a time, beating until thick and pale yellow. Add the vanilla. Gradually add the milk.

Sift together the flour and baking powder, and fold into the egg mixture, mixing until just combined. Pour the batter evenly into the prepared cake pans and bake for 35 to 40 minutes or until a cake tester comes out clean when inserted into the center of the cakes. Cool the cakes in their pans for

10 minutes, then invert them onto wire racks to cool completely.

To prepare the filling, cut off the top, bottom, and prickly skin of the pineapple. Cut the pineapple lengthwise into quarters and remove the core. Finely chop the pineapple. Reserve 2 cups in a nonmetallic bowl until ready to assemble the cake.

To prepare a fresh coconut for the topping, use a nail to puncture the three eyes at the end of the coconut; drain the milk into a bowl and reserve for another use. Using a hammer, take a few gentle whacks at the coconut to split the shell of the nut. Remove the flesh and peel the brown skin with a vegetable peeler. Run each piece of coconut across the large holes of a grater, creating long shaved pieces of coconut about ¼ inch wide. Keep the coconut pieces tightly wrapped in the refrigerator until ready to use.

To make the icing, in a small heavy saucepan combine the water with the sugar. Stir over medium heat until all the sugar is dissolved. Be careful not to boil or brown the syrup as this will discolor the icing. When the liquid has become a syrup, remove the pan from the heat and cool slightly.

In the bowl of an electric mixer, beat the egg whites on high speed until fluffy. Continue beating and slowly pour the warm syrup into the egg whites. Add the vanilla. Reduce the speed to medium and continue beating the mixture until it is smooth and very thick in consistency.

To assemble the cake, place one layer on a serving plate or cake stand. Cover with icing and top with a layer of half the pineapple. Repeat this with the next layer, then place the third layer on top. Spread the remaining icing over the top and sides of the cake. Sprinkle the sides and top of the cake with the shredded coconut, pressing it gently into the frosting.

Keep the cake in a cool, dark place, covered, until ready to serve. If you refrigerate the cake, cover it loosely with plastic wrap.

left: *I received this giant glass cake dome as a present. The green enamel base was located in Sag Harbor, and the marriage of the two was surprisingly perfect. This cake should be covered so that the icing doesn't crystallize in the air.* right: *Custard pies are another Southern favorite, and this thin, rich tart, made with buttermilk, lemon, and coconut, is really good.*

Banana Ginger Custard DELIGHT

Serves 10

Soft, puffy gingersnap cookies are the base for this wonderful banana custard. Since this menu has two other desserts, I've figured the recipe for only 10 servings. But you can double the ingredients if you want; you'll have enough cookies.

Custard

    2 cups milk
    4 large egg yolks
 ¼ cup sugar
 ⅛ teaspoon salt
    1 teaspoon vanilla extract

Meringue

    4 large egg whites
       Pinch of salt
    1 cup sugar

 20 Gingersnap Cookies (recipe
       follows) or store-bought
    2 bananas

To make the custard, scald the milk and allow it to cool slightly.

In a medium mixing bowl, lightly beat the egg yolks, adding the sugar and the salt. Beat the mixture until the sugar and salt are dissolved.

Slowly add the scalded milk to the egg mixture, whisking constantly. Immediately transfer the egg mixture to the top half of a double boiler and cook over simmering water. Stir the custard until it begins to thicken and coats the back of a spoon. Immediately remove from the heat.

Transfer the custard to a clean bowl and continue whisking for 2 minutes. Add in the vanilla, and refrigerate uncovered for 20 to 25 minutes, until barely warm.

above: *The recipe for gingersnap cookies makes lots of them, but served in the banana custard dessert or out of a cookie jar, these snaps are popular.*
opposite: *I found a lot of yellow custard cups one summer as I rummaged around thrift shops and flea markets. They're just right for this dessert; the high meringue and the pudding within cook wonderfully.*

While the custard is cooling, make the meringue topping for the dessert. In the bowl of an electric mixer on high speed, beat the egg whites until they are thick and foamy. Sprinkle in salt and add the sugar, ¼ cup at a time, beating the egg whites until they are stiff and glossy.

To assemble, preheat the oven to 300° F. Place a gingersnap cookie in the bottom of each of 10 individual custard cups. Fill the cups ¾ full with the barely warm custard. Slice the bananas; top each cup with a layer of banana slices and a second gingersnap cookie. Mound the meringue on top of each cup, making sure to spread the meringue all the way to the rim of the cup so that it doesn't shrink. Bake for 5 minutes, or until the meringue turns slightly golden.

Gingersnap COOKIES

Makes 5 dozen 2-inch cookies

 3¾ cups unbleached all-purpose
       flour
    3 teaspoons baking soda
    2 teaspoons ground ginger
    1 teaspoon ground cinnamon
 ½ teaspoon ground cloves
 ¾ cup (1½ sticks) unsalted
       butter, at room temperature
    2 cups dark brown sugar
    2 large eggs, well beaten
 ½ cup dark molasses
    2 teaspoons fresh lime juice
    1 teaspoon vanilla extract
       Sugar for sprinkling

In a large bowl, sift together the flour, baking soda, ginger, cinnamon, and cloves. In the bowl of an electric mixer, cream together the butter and brown sugar on medium speed until creamy.

Add the eggs, beating until fluffy. Add the molasses, lime juice, and vanilla. Continue beating until well combined. Gradually add the flour mixture, beating as little as possible.

Divide the dough into two portions; wrap in plastic wrap and chill for at least 1 hour. (The dough can be made a few days in advance and kept in the refrigerator.)

Preheat the oven to 350° F. Line baking sheets with parchment paper.

Using your hands, roll the dough into ¾-inch balls and place them on the baking sheets. Sprinkle each cookie with sugar and bake for 10 minutes. Transfer the cookies to a baking rack to cool. The cookies will keep for a few days in an airtight container.

NORTH CAROLINA Barbecue

Serves 16

✳ *Mint* Juleps

Roquefort Potato Salad ✳ *Hush Puppies*

North Carolina *Pork* Barbecue

Kitty Murphy's *Brunswick Stew*

✳ Red Green *Slaw*

Peach and *Nectarine* Cobbler

NORTH CAROLINA Barbecue

MY FRIEND ZACKI MURPHY AND I HAVE LONG DISCUSSED THE VERY CONTROVERSIAL SUBJECT OF BARBECUE. BOTH OF US HAVE JUDGED THE ANNUAL MEMPHIS BARBECUE CONTEST WHERE, IN MAY, COOKS FROM ALL OVER AMERICA CONVENE TO COMPETE IN WHAT IS REPUTEDLY THE WORLD'S BIGGEST BARBECUE GET-TOGETHER. I JUDGED THE "WHOLE HOG" LAST TIME I WAS THERE, AND ZACKI PRESIDED OVER THE RIBS. WHAT WE'VE BOTH CONCLUDED IS THAT NORTH CAROLINA BARBECUE IS OUR FAVORITE AND THAT ZACKI'S VERSION IS SUPERIOR. WHILE IT IS IMPOSSIBLE TO RE-CREATE THE FLAVOR OF LEXINGTON BARBECUE AT HOME, THE FOLLOWING RECIPE IS AS CLOSE AN APPROXIMATION AS ONE CAN GET WITHOUT THE EXACT LOCAL HICKORY WOOD. USING HICKORY CUT FROM MY OWN TREES, ALONG WITH A NORMAL OUTDOOR COVERED GRILL OR SMOKER, WE HAD GREAT SUCCESS IN EMULATING WHAT WE CONSIDER GREAT BARBECUE. WHAT MAKES THIS MENU ADDITIONALLY DELICIOUS ARE ALL THE HOMEMADE "PICKLES." I HAVE COLLECTED RECIPES FROM EVERYWHERE IN THE SOUTH FOR VINEGAR-PICKLED OKRA, HARD-BOILED "CAYENNE" EGGS, JERUSALEM ARTICHOKE PICKLES, CORN RELISH, CAULIFLOWER PICKLES, AND TWICE-DONE SWEET-AND-SOUR PICKLES. I LOVE THIS KIND OF FOOD FOR OUTDOOR ENTERTAINING ANYWHERE, BUT IT IS EQUALLY GOOD SERVED AROUND A KITCHEN TABLE WITH PITCHERS OF MINT JULIPS OR ICED TEA, AND LOTS OF COLD BEER.

previous page: *It is traditional to serve mint juleps in tall, icy, monogrammed silver tumblers. However, for an informal luncheon such as this, old gold-rimmed glass tumblers work very well. Sugar-crusted rims make these drinks taste even better.* above: *The shredded pork barbecue on its soft hamburger roll makes a perfect lunch-size sandwich. For this gathering I used beige restaurant dishes.*

Mint JULEPS

Makes 16 drinks

What a treat to be served a frosty glass of mint julep as a special beginning to a North Carolina feast. Plan one generous drink per person.

17 lemons
3½ cups sugar
 3 cups water
32 sprigs of mint
    Ice cubes
6–8 cups sour mash bourbon

Squeeze 16 of the lemons, reserving the rinds.

In a small heavy saucepan dissolve 3 cups of the sugar into the water, then add the lemon rinds and cook over medium heat until the liquid becomes syrupy, approximately 15 minutes. Cool to room temperature.

Place the remaining ½ cup of sugar on a small plate. Cut the remaining lemon into quarters. Rub the wedges along the rims of 16 tall glasses and invert the glasses in the sugar to create a sugared rim.

Crush a mint sprig into the bottom of each glass with a wooden reamer. Fill each glass with ice cubes and divide the lemon juice and syrup equally among the glasses. Top off with about ½ cup of bourbon per glass. Garnish each glass with a fresh sprig of mint.

Roquefort
POTATO SALAD

Serves 16

Roquefort cheese has a unique flavor. It is my favorite blue cheese and I always buy the real French variety.

5 pounds small red potatoes, scrubbed
½ cup dry white vermouth
¾ cup safflower oil
⅔ cup apple cider vinegar
3 teaspoons Tabasco sauce
3 tablespoons sugar
3 tablespoons grainy mustard
3 garlic cloves, minced
1 teaspoon cumin
1 tablespoon celery seed
6 scallions, chopped
1 orange bell pepper, seeded and diced
   Salt and freshly ground pepper
6 large leaves fresh basil
6 ounces Roquefort cheese, crumbled

Place the potatoes in a large pot and cover with cold water. Bring to a boil over high heat and immediately reduce to a simmer, cooking the potatoes until tender when pricked with a fork, about 20 minutes. Don't overcook.

Drain the potatoes well, cool slightly, and cut in half. While they are still warm, toss the potatoes in a large bowl with the vermouth.

In a medium bowl, whisk together the safflower oil, vinegar, Tabasco, sugar, mustard, garlic, cumin, and celery seed. Gently stir in the scallions and orange pepper. Pour the dressing over the potatoes. Season with salt and pepper to taste.

Make a chiffonade of the basil by placing the leaves directly one on top of another in the same direction. Starting along one edge, roll the leaves lengthwise. Using a very sharp knife, cut the rolled basil into thin pieces. Sprinkle the basil over the potatoes, add the crumbled Roquefort cheese, and toss.

This potato salad can be made a day in advance and kept covered in the refrigerator. But it is best served right away.

HUSH PUPPIES

Serves 16

Well made, hush puppies can be light and delicious. They can be served as an hors d'oeuvre with cocktails, or fried in batches during dinner.

1 large egg
1 cup buttermilk
1 pound white cornmeal
1 tablespoon coarse salt
¼ teaspoon freshly ground pepper
1 tablespoon sugar
¼ teaspoon baking soda
1 scallion, sliced thin
4 cups vegetable oil for frying
   Seven-pepper jelly

In a medium bowl, whisk together the egg and buttermilk. Stir in the white cornmeal, salt, pepper, sugar, baking soda, and scallion. Don't overmix.

In a heavy medium pot, heat the vegetable oil over medium-high heat to 375° F., regulating the temperature of the oil so that it never reaches the point of smoking. Using two small spoons, scoop up enough batter to fill one spoon and use the other spoon to ease the dough off into the oil. Fry the hush puppies 3 to 4 minutes, turning once with a slotted spoon to brown evenly. Drain on paper towels. Serve hot with a seven-pepper jelly.

left: *Some of the Southern flour mills offer premixed hush puppy, biscuit, and cornbread mixes that can help make the preparation of this meal easier.* below: *I have covered many tables in East Hampton with stainless galvanized steel or tin-coated steel sheeting. Wooden tables thus protected can be left out in the rain. The steel actually looks better a year after it has been exposed to the elements. Here, the table is set with heavy restaurant plates, a variety of greenware bowls, red and black napkins, which I made by the score for meals such as this, and a long French linen-lined baguette basket for the hot hush puppies.*

above: *Use young red potatoes in the salad. They cook tender without getting mushy, and keep their shape even after being dressed.* below: *Crush mint in the bottom of each glass to release its powerful taste. The crushed mint gets dark, so garnish the drink with a fresh sprig.*

below: *Vegetable pickles such as these Jerusalem artichokes require processing for a few minutes to ensure a tight seal. After a six-week rest to absorb the pickling flavors, they become crispy and very tasty.*

left: *One perfect hush puppy. Serve them piping hot with a spoonful of hot pepper jelly, or a dash of Tabasco if you choose. Little bowls of pickles and relishes should be placed around the table. I use pottery custard cups for these garnishes.*

North Carolina
PORK BARBECUE

Serves 16

I always make twice as much of this as I need because the cooked meat freezes very well. Buy fresh pork shoulder, choosing lean over fat. Well-aged hickory wood or store-bought hickory chips give this barbecue its unique and savory flavoring. The vinegar-based sauce is uniquely North Carolina and is very addictive. Watch out!

2   10-pound pork shoulders, with bone
Hickory chips and charcoal for grilling, in a 50:50 ratio
2   cups white wine vinegar
⅔   cup ketchup
⅓   cup sugar
¼   cup honey
½   teaspoon cayenne pepper
½   teaspoon coarse salt
1   teaspoon freshly ground pepper
16   soft hamburger buns, split
Red Green Slaw (page 79)

Preheat the oven to 500° F.

Wrap the pork shoulders in aluminum foil and place in a large heavy roasting pan. Roast the pork shoulders for 20 minutes at 500°, then reduce the heat to 250° and cook for an additional 5 hours, turning them every hour.

Using a covered grill, start the fire 1 hour before the pork shoulders are finished roasting, using the mixture of hickory chips and charcoal. When the pork shoulders are roasted, remove the foil and transfer them to the grill. Cover the grill and smoke the pork for 20 to 40 minutes.

Allow the meat to cool so it can be handled, then transfer it to a large bowl. Remove the meat from the bone and using your fingers, finely shred the

Every August and September, my eighty-year-old mother Martha and I put up dozens of quarts of our own tomatoes. Using them over the cold months is almost like picking them fresh again, right from the backyard garden. I sometimes add fresh basil leaves or sprigs of fresh thyme to the jars.

meat. Wrap half the meat in plastic wrap and aluminum foil and freeze for later use.

In a medium saucepan, mix together the vinegar, ketchup, sugar, honey, cayenne pepper, salt, and pepper. Simmer the sauce ingredients for 10 minutes over low heat. Reserve ½ cup of sauce and pour the remaining sauce over the meat and toss until the meat is evenly coated. Keep the meat warm in a double boiler until ready to serve.

To serve, spoon a portion of meat onto the bottom of a soft bun, mound the Red Green Slaw on top of it, and pour a little of the remaining sauce over all, then top with the second half of the bun.

The meat can be made a day or two in advance and kept in an airtight container in the refrigerator. To serve, reheat it in the top of a double boiler over simmering, not boiling, water.

Kitty Murphy's
BRUNSWICK STEW

Serves 16

Zacki's mom, Kitty, has perfected her version of this delightful concoction for more than six decades, and she graciously allowed us to improvise on her original.

3   4-pound whole broiler chickens
1   quart chicken stock, or broth
2   quarts water
Salt and freshly ground pepper
½   pound thick cut bacon, cut into 2-inch pieces and cooked
6   large yellow onions, chopped coarsely
6   garlic cloves, peeled and cut in half
6   large ripe tomatoes, peeled, seeded, and quartered
18   Yellow Finn potatoes, peeled and diced
6   cups fresh lima beans or 3 10-ounce packages frozen
8   ears corn, husked and cut into 1-inch rounds
3   tablespoons Worcestershire sauce
6   tablespoons (¾ stick) unsalted butter

In a large shallow pot, simmer the chickens with the chicken stock, water, and salt and pepper over low heat until they are tender, about 1 hour. Skim the broth often.

Remove the chickens from the pot to a bowl to cool. Return the broth to the stove, increase the heat to high, and reduce the broth by one quarter. Return the heat to low and continue to simmer.

Remove and discard the skin and bones from the chickens, keeping the meat in pieces as large as possible. Return the chicken meat to the broth and add the bacon, onions, garlic, tomatoes, potatoes, and lima beans (only if using fresh) and simmer for 1 hour, constantly skimming the pot.

If you are using frozen lima beans, make sure they are defrosted and add them at the end with the corn and Worcestershire sauce. Simmer an additional 10 minutes and add the butter to the pot, allowing it to melt into the stew. Serve immediately.

Red Green SLAW

Serves 16

Soft buns and ketchup-colored slaw—indispensable accompaniments for barbecue. Flavor the slaw well and mound it generously atop the shredded beef.

¾ cup ketchup
⅓ cup apple cider vinegar
½ cup sugar
½ teaspoon coarse salt
½ teaspoon freshly ground pepper
2½ pounds green cabbage, shredded

In a large mixing bowl, whisk together the ketchup, vinegar, sugar, salt, and pepper. Add the cabbage and toss until well coated with the sauce.

The slaw can be made a few hours in advance and kept covered in the refrigerator until ready to use.

above: *The barbecue sandwiches were served in a napkin-lined bowl, a whole pile of them ready to eat.* right: *Colorful, fresh, and rather light, with a clear broth, this Brunswick stew is more like a hearty soup than a stew. Serve it right from a shallow cooking pot (spattered enamel would be nice) or from a wide shallow bowl like this one of yellow pottery.*

Peach and Nectarine COBBLER

Makes two 8- or 10-inch cobblers

As a substitute for the nectarine-peach combination, try plums and mixed berries, or pears and apples.

Crust

2½ cups unbleached all-purpose flour

3 tablespoons sugar

1 cup (2 sticks) unsalted butter, chilled and cut into small pieces

4 tablespoons ice water

2 large egg yolks, lightly beaten

Filling

14 nectarines

14 peaches

8 tablespoons vanilla sugar (see Note)

4 tablespoons (½ stick) butter

Preheat the oven to 375° F. Butter two 8- or 10-inch round baking dishes.

Combine the flour and sugar in the bowl of a food processor. All ingredients should be cold. Add the chilled butter in pieces and process for approximately 10 seconds, or until the mixture resembles coarse meal. (To mix by hand, combine the dry ingredients in a large mixing bowl. Using a pastry blender or two table knives, cut in the butter until the mixture resembles coarse meal.)

While the machine is running, add the ice water, a few drops at a time, along with the egg yolks, one at a time, through the feed tube, just until the dough holds together without being wet or sticky. Do not overprocess; 30 seconds should be sufficient. Test the dough at this point by squeezing a small amount together. If it is too crumbly, add a bit more water.

Divide the dough into two equal amounts. Place each on a piece of plastic wrap and press the dough into a flat circle with your fists. (This makes rolling easier than if the pastry is chilled as a ball.) Wrap and chill well, at least 1 hour.

Wash and dry the fruit. Cut into wedges and evenly distribute between the two prepared baking dishes. Sprinkle the fruit with 3 tablespoons of the vanilla sugar per dish and dot with the butter, 2 tablespoons per dish.

Roll out each piece of dough large enough to cover the top of each baking dish. Place the dough over the fruit and pinch around the edge of the baking dish to seal. Trim the excess dough. Make 4 or 5 slits in the dough to allow the steam to escape and divide the remaining sugar, sprinkling it over the top of each crust. Bake for 45 minutes until the crust is golden brown. Serve warm or cooled.

Note: To make vanilla sugar, store 6 to 8 fresh vanilla beans in a covered quart jar filled with white sugar. Replenish the sugar as you use it.

opposite: *I baked the fruit cobblers in the bottoms of Moroccan tagines, which have high sides and broad edges to prevent overflows and dripping fruit juices. The very plain pastry crust sprinkled with sugar is excellent with the seasonal fruit.*
above: *More restaurant dishes for coffee: little demitasse cups and saucers. I used a very good coffee from Louisiana called Community and prepared it in a terrific enamel drip pot, a gift to me from the Parlange family of Baton Rouge. Strong dripped Southern coffee is served with sweetened boiled milk, poured into the cup half and half.*
below: *Part of my Bakelite flatware collection includes bi-colored handles such as these. This flatware is funky and decorative, and it lasts for ages as long as you don't put it into the dishwasher.*

Crabs AND Corn *on the Beach*

Serves 8

Orange-Lime *Margaritas*

Crab Cakes ✳ Spicy Blue *Crab* Boil

Corn on the Cob

Strawberry Shortbread Cakes

Strawberry Pie ✳

Crabs AND *Corn* *on the Beach*

MY FRIENDS BEN AND BONNIE KRUPINSKI HAVE AN UNUSUAL LIVING ARRANGEMENT. IN ONE LITTLE LONG ISLAND VILLAGE THEY HAVE THE BEST OF TWO WORLDS: AN INLAND HOUSE AND A SEASIDE HOUSE. MOSTLY THEY SLEEP IN THE INLAND HOUSE, BUT ON WEEKENDS ALL YEAR ROUND, THEY ENTERTAIN IN THE SEASIDE HOUSE. WITH CLEAR WATERS AND A GENTLE BREEZE, THIS SPECIAL SPOT LENDS ITSELF TO THE SIMPLEST MODE OF CELEBRATING THE PLEASURES OF GOOD FOOD AND DRINK. FRESHNESS IS KEY: THE INGREDIENTS FOR THIS FEAST WERE ALL LOCAL AND ALL VERY FRESH. THE CRABS WERE CAUGHT THAT MORNING IN ONE OF THE TIDAL PONDS ON THE EAST END. THE CORN WAS PICKED THAT AFTERNOON ON THE NORTH FORK. THE CRAB CAKES WERE MADE FROM FRESHLY PICKED BLUE CRAB FROM THE BRIDGEHAMPTON SEAFOOD SHOP, AND THE STRAWBERRIES WERE FROM AN EAST HAMPTON FARM. THIS TYPE OF MEAL CAN BE MADE FOR ANY NUMBER OF GUESTS. IT IS ALL ABOUT MULTIPLICATION. ALLOW SIX TO EIGHT CRABS PER PERSON, THREE CRAB CAKES, AND TWO TO THREE EARS OF CORN. DESSERTS SHOULD BE MADE IN QUANTITY: AT LEAST ONE PIE FOR EVERY EIGHT GUESTS. A WARM AND SUNNY DAY IS BEST FOR THIS SORT OF OUTDOOR FEAST, BUT A PROTECTED PORCH OR DECK OR A NEWSPAPER-COVERED KITCHEN TABLE WILL DO JUST AS WELL ON A RAINY DAY.

previous page: *A sturdy teak table and heavy, comfortable armchairs were great set on the sandy beach for this sit-down feast. Crabs take a long time to pound and pick and you should plan for a long, leisurely get-together. Napkins that are really towels, along with hot terry-cloth washcloths to wipe spicy fingers, and pitchers or bottles of ice-cold beer are absolute musts for this meal.*

above: *Once the crabs and corn are boiled, they are set out on the paper-covered table to be devoured by the hungry guests. In keeping with the tradition of the great crab restaurants, I give everyone a small wooden mallet with which to crack the shells.*

clockwise from top left: *My daughter, Alexis, started collecting Depression "Ring" glasses several years ago. She has given me lots of this and that, including these generously sized cocktail glasses. With salt-encrusted rims they make the perfect margarita glass. Blue hard-shell crabs are in season in the Northeast from May to December. When mature they weigh about 6 ounces. I like to go crabbing with strings and pieces of chicken as bait, but to catch enough crabs for a crowd takes quite a while. After the corn is boiled I sprinkle it while still hot with coarse salt and pile it in an enamel basin. For a crab boil, I like to put lots of paper on the table so that messy layers can be peeled off as the meal proceeds. Crab cakes are served piping hot out of the pan.*

Crabs AND Corn

Orange-Lime MARGARITAS

Makes 4

For the best flavor, I use fresh limes and oranges, Tres Generaciones tequila, and Grand Marnier or Cointreau liqueur.

- 1 cup water
- 2 cups sugar
  - Chipped ice
- 1 cup fresh lime juice
- 1 cup fresh orange juice
- 1 cup tequila
- ½ cup orange liqueur
- 1 lime
- ¼ cup coarse salt

In a small heavy saucepan, combine the water and sugar. Cook over medium heat until it forms a clear syrup, about 10 minutes. Set aside and allow the syrup to cool completely.

Fill a large pitcher half full with chipped ice; stir in the lime juice, orange juice, sugar syrup, tequila, and orange liqueur.

Cut the lime into 8 wedges. Using a wedge of lime, rub the rims of four glasses with the lime and invert the glasses into a plate of coarse salt. Fill each glass with chipped ice and pour the margarita mix, evenly divided, over the ice. Garnish each drink with a wedge of lime.

Double the quantities and use 2 pitchers to serve 8.

Crab CAKES

Serves 8

Use jumbo lump crabmeat for the flakiest and tastiest of crab cakes.

- 1 cup dried bread crumbs
- 2 large eggs, lightly beaten
- 2 pounds lump crabmeat, picked over for cartilage

- ½ cup fresh cilantro leaves, chopped
- 4 scallions, chopped
- 1 red bell pepper, seeded and diced
- 1 yellow bell pepper, seeded and diced
- 1 jalapeño pepper, seeded and diced
- 1 cup mayonnaise
  - Salt and freshly ground pepper
- 1 cup vegetable oil for frying

In a large bowl, gently mix together the bread crumbs, eggs, crabmeat, cilantro, scallions, peppers, mayonnaise, and salt and pepper to taste.

Form the crab meat mixture into 24 small, thick cakes, about 2 inches in diameter. Heat the vegetable oil in a large frying pan over medium-high heat until hot, not smoking. Cook the crab cakes for 2 to 3 minutes per side, until golden brown, turning them with a spatula. Drain them on a plate lined with a paper towel before serving. Serve hot.

Spicy BLUE CRAB BOIL

Serves 8

Rubber hammers or wooden mallets can be used to crack the crab shells; make sure to tap lightly so that the meat, instead of being crushed, can be removed in large chunks.

- 1 bushel (about 48) live hard-shell blue crabs, well washed
- 1 1-pound package Obrycki's Spice (see Note)

Cover the live crabs with ice for about 15 minutes to sedate them.

Fill an old-fashioned steamer pot with water and bring to a boil over

high heat or a hot fire. Layer the crabs with the spice mix in the steamer basket and cover. Steam the crabs for about 10 minutes over boiling water, then turn off the heat and let the crabs sit undisturbed in the covered pot for another 20 minutes. The crabs will be bright red and slightly crusty with spices; do not brush off the spices.

Turn the crabs onto a surface covered with paper and eat hot or warm.

Note: Obrycki's Spice is a secret blend of spices containing black pepper, salt, dry mustard, cayenne pepper, and other seasonings. It and the mallets are available by mail order from Obrycki's Crab House, 1727 East Pratt Street, Baltimore, Maryland 21231. (800) 742-1741.

CORN *on the Cob*

Serves 8

A bowl of melted butter, flavored with lime juice and cayenne pepper if you like, should be placed within reach of every guest.

- 2 dozen ears fresh corn, husked
- 2 tablespoons sugar
- 1 cup (2 sticks) butter, melted
  - Juice of 3 limes (optional)
- ¾ teaspoon cayenne pepper (optional)
  - Coarse salt

Bring a large stockpot of water to a rapid boil over high heat. Add the sugar and the corn and cook for 8 to 10 minutes. The corn is done when all of a sudden the sweet smell of corn permeates the air.

Remove the corn from the water with tongs, brush with butter (seasoned with lime juice and cayenne pepper if you wish), and sprinkle with coarse salt. Serve immediately.

Strawberry SHORTBREAD CAKES

Serves 8

Roll the dough on a generously sugared board. The sugar makes the shortbread crusty and crunchy.

1 cup (2 sticks) unsalted butter, at room temperature
½ cup confectioners' sugar, sifted
2 cups unbleached all-purpose flour
¼ teaspoon salt
2 quarts strawberries, washed and hulled
2 tablespoons granulated sugar
2 cups heavy cream
1 teaspoon vanilla extract
¼ cup melted, cooled apple jelly

Preheat the oven to 350° F. Line a baking sheet with parchment paper.

In the bowl of an electric mixer, cream the butter until fluffy, about 2 minutes. Gradually add the confectioners' sugar and beat until well combined. Add the flour and salt, mixing until just combined. Do not overmix.

On a well-sugared surface, roll out the dough ¼ inch thick. Using a 4½-inch fluted biscuit cutter, cut the dough into rounds and transfer them to the baking sheet with a large spatula. Bake the shortbread for 20 to 25 minutes. It should be somewhat firm, but still pale in color. Cool on a rack.

While the shortbread is baking, cut the strawberries in half and toss them in a large bowl with the sugar. Allow them to sit at least 30 minutes.

When ready to serve, beat the cream, vanilla, and apple jelly with an electric mixer until stiff. (The bowl, beaters, and cream should be well chilled before whipping.) To assemble, cover one cookie with strawberries and a layer of whipped cream. Top

Strawberry pie must be made from small berries that are especially dense. A watery, insipid berry will make a nondescript pie.

the whipped cream with another cookie, then layer again with strawberries and whipped cream.

Note: The pectin in the apple jelly prevents the whipped cream from "weeping," and it adds a natural sweetness.

Strawberry PIE

Makes one 10-inch pie

For this pie the strawberries should be so deliciously juicy that a bit of flour must be added to the fruit before baking.

½ recipe Martha's Sweet Pie Crust (recipe follows)
2 quarts strawberries, washed, hulled, and cut in half
½ cup sugar
1–2 tablespoons flour
   Juice of 1 lemon
   Whipped cream, for garnish

Preheat the oven to 375° F.

On a lightly floured surface, roll out the pie dough approximately 4 inches larger than the pie pan.

Line the pan with the dough, allow-ing the excess to hang over the sides. Spoon in the strawberries. Sprinkle them with the sugar, flour, and lemon juice. Fold the excess dough over the berries toward the pie's center.

Bake for 45 to 60 minutes until the pastry is golden brown. Allow the pie to cool. Serve with whipped cream.

Martha's SWEET PIE CRUST

Makes two 8- to 10-inch pie crusts

Folding the edges over the berries keeps the juices in the pie.

2½ cups unbleached all-purpose flour
¼ teaspoon salt
3 tablespoons sugar
1 cup (2 sticks) unsalted butter, chilled and cut into small pieces
4 tablespoons ice water
2 large egg yolks, lightly beaten

Put the flour, salt, and sugar in the bowl of a food processor. All ingredients should be cold. Add the butter and process for 10 seconds, or just until the mixture resembles coarse meal. (To mix by hand, combine the dry ingredients in a large mixing bowl. Using a pastry blender or two table knives, cut in the butter until the mixture resembles coarse meal.)

Add the ice water bit by bit, alternating with the egg yolks; process just until the dough holds together without being wet or sticky. Do not overprocess. Test the dough by squeezing a small amount together. If it is too dry and crumbly, add a bit more water.

Divide the dough in half and form into two discs. Wrap each well and chill for at least an hour.

right: *This isn't the kind of food that goes well with damask napkins or fine china, so we used large linen dish towels in a very pale beige with red stripes. The desserts were served on Fire King plates. I whipped a good quantity of heavy cream from a local dairy, and sweetened it slightly with a bit of sugar.*

below: *Shortbread is the basis for this most delectable dessert. The shortbread cookies are layered with heavy cream, whipped thick, and fresh strawberries that have been sliced and macerated in sugar.*

Tuscan Buffet *Outdoors*

Serves 20

Eggplant with Roasted *Tomato* Purée

✳ Miniature *Cauliflower* with Bread Crumbs

Small Vegetables Filled with Seasoned *Pork* ✳ Pickled *Eggplant*

Roasted Tomatoes Topped with *White Beans*

Roasted *Peppers* with a Variety of Fillings

Grilled Cipolla *Onions* in Balsamic Vinegar Sauce

Stuffed Roly-Poly *Zucchini* ✳

Wine-Poached Summer *Fruits*

Tuscan Buffet *Outdoors*

FOR MY FRIEND ZACKI'S BIRTHDAY, I ENTERTAINED A GROUP OF CLOSE FRIENDS AND SERVED THIS TUSCAN BUFFET. IN A STONE-WALLED SECTION OF MY HERB GARDEN, NARROW PIECES OF CEDAR SHINGLE WERE INSERTED BETWEEN STONES OF THE WALL TO SERVE AS LITTLE "SHELVES" FOR VOTIVE CANDLES. ALL EVENING I WAS REMINDED OF WONDERFUL PARTIES I HAD ATTENDED IN ITALY, IN CAMAIORE AND LUCCA AND FLORENCE. EACH RECIPE WAS INSPIRED BY A DISH I HAD EATEN ON THOSE SUMMER TRIPS: YOUNG CAULIFLOWER WITH BREAD CRUMBS, STUFFED PEPPERS, ROASTED TOMATOES, AND WINE-INFUSED SUMMER FRUITS. THE DISTINCTIVE RUSTIC FLAVORS OF TUSCANY LEND THEMSELVES TO EITHER AN INDOOR OR OUTDOOR PRESENTATION; THIS MENU CAN BE SERVED IN A ROMANTIC EVENING SETTING, AS IT WAS HERE, OR ON A SUNNY TERRACE AT LUNCH. FOR A SMALLER GROUP OF GUESTS, THE NUMBER OF DISHES CAN BE REDUCED WITH LITTLE IMPACT ON THE WHOLE MEAL. HOWEVER, I LIKE THE VARIETY AND THE CHOICE OF A GENEROUS BUFFET MENU. WHEN ONE WALKS INTO A SIMPLE RESTAURANT IN ITALY, SIMILAR PLATTERS OF FOOD ARE OFTEN SET OUT FOR VIEW. EVERYTHING LOOKS AND SMELLS SO GOOD IT IS DIFFICULT TO CHOOSE! THAT IS WHY A MEAL SUCH AS THIS SHOULD BE LEISURELY, ENJOYED WITH GOOD WINE AND GOOD COMPANY.

previous page: *Tuscan dishes call for the very freshest, ripest fruits and vegetables.* above: *My "grotto" is really the stone-walled area under the cantilevered porch of my barn. The floor is bluestone, and the "ceiling" (actually the underside of the deck) is rustic wood. I can set up to four tables comfortably in this spot, which opens onto the fragrant beds of the herb garden. For my Tuscan buffet I used beige linen cloths with saffron linen toppers; the beige linen napkins were homemade. To create a simple, appealing place setting, I used vitreous china that originally was made for diners. Flowerpots planted with various plants, citron and yellow Depression goblets, and yellow Bakelite flatware complemented the setting. Votive candles illuminated the place nicely.*

left: *Burpee's 'Purple Blush' egg-plant is a pale opalescent lavender version of the usual dark blackish purple vegetable. The flesh is very white and does not have the expected bitterness of the common types. I first saw this Violetta in Lucca, where I ate it pickled, stuffed, roasted, and fried. The pale green squash is spaghetti squash, a wonderful vegetable whose flesh cooks into spaghetti-like strands.*

above: *In the summertime, look for small fresh cauliflower. These are excellent steamed tender and topped with fresh butter-browned bread crumbs. Even the leaves of the cauli-flower taste good steamed in this way. The dish is quintessentially Tuscan in its utter simplicity, proof, if any was needed, that sophistication does not mean fussiness.*

Pickled EGGPLANT

Serves 20

Soaking the eggplant removes any bitter taste. Violetta eggplants have less of this inherent bitterness and need less soaking before being pickled in vinegar brine. This recipe can be made a day or two in advance of the party.

1 large eggplant, preferably
    Violetta, peeled and julienned
3 bay leaves
¼ cup rice vinegar
2 tablespoons sugar
¼ cup water
¼ cup basil leaves

Fill a large saucepan three-quarters full with water and bring to a boil over high heat. Add the eggplant and bay leaves. Remove the saucepan from the heat and soak for 30 minutes. Drain the eggplant well in a colander.

In a medium bowl, mix together the rice vinegar, sugar, and water. Add the eggplant and toss well. Allow the eggplant to marinate at least 2 to 3 hours. Right before serving, sprinkle with basil leaves.

EGGPLANT *with Roasted Tomato Purée*

Serves 20

Roasted tomatoes are a summer treat. They can be served peeled and seeded as a side dish, or puréed into a sauce.

2 large eggplants
    Coarse salt
½ cup pine nuts
2 large tomatoes
½ cup plus 2 tablespoons
    extra-virgin olive oil

2 large onions, chopped
2 garlic cloves, crushed
¼ cup fresh parsley, chopped
1 tablespoon Worcestershire sauce
    Freshly ground pepper

Preheat the oven to 300° F.

Slice the eggplants into ½-inch-thick rounds. Place the rounds on a clean kitchen towel and sprinkle them with salt to leach out any bitterness and excess water. Allow them to sit for 30 minutes. Rinse the slices in cold water and pat them dry with a towel.

On a baking sheet, spread the pine nuts evenly and toast in the preheated oven for 5 to 8 minutes. Shake the sheet often to ensure even toasting. The nuts are toasted when you can first smell them; be careful not to burn. Set aside to cool.

Roast the tomatoes by skewering them with a long fork and holding them over the flame of a gas burner, turning until the skin blackens. You can also roast them in an oven preheated to 500° F. Slice the tomatoes in half, place cut side up on a baking sheet lined with parchment paper, drizzle with olive oil, and roast for 30 minutes. When cool enough to handle, shake out the seeds, remove the skins, and chop coarsely. Drain in a sieve, reserving the juice.

In a large sauté pan, heat 2 tablespoons of the olive oil. Add the onions and sauté over medium-high heat for 5 minutes, until soft. Add the crushed garlic and sauté for 1 minute. Then add the tomatoes, parsley, Worcestershire sauce, and salt and pepper to taste. Continue sautéing until all the liquid has evaporated, about 2 minutes. Transfer the tomato mixture to a food processor or food mill and purée until smooth.

In a large frying pan, heat the ½ cup of olive oil and the reserved tomato juice over medium heat. Add the eggplant slices, cooking in batches to avoid overcrowding, and poach for 5 minutes on each side, or until the slices are tender all the way through. Remove the slices with a slotted spoon as they are cooked and drain on paper towels.

Serve warm or at room temperature with the roasted tomato purée. Sprinkle with the toasted pine nuts.

Miniature CAULIFLOWER *with Bread Crumbs*

Serves 20

Tiny cauliflower are a very nice version of one of my favorite vegetables.

6 small, very young cauliflower
½ cup fine bread crumbs
3 tablespoons unsalted butter

Cut the stem of each cauliflower off at the base, so that the cauliflower head will stand upright. Cut an X in the bottom of each stem to quicken the cooking time.

Place a rack in the bottom of a large stockpot and add 1 inch of water. Bring the water to a boil over high heat and place the cauliflowers on the rack. Cover the pot and steam until tender, about 15 minutes.

Remove the cauliflowers from the pot and allow the heads to drain in a colander for a few minutes.

Melt the butter in a skillet over medium heat. Add the bread crumbs and cook until the crumbs are nut brown. Do not burn.

Sprinkle the bread crumbs evenly over the cauliflower heads. Serve hot or at room temperature.

Small
VEGETABLES
Filled with
SEASONED PORK

Serves 20

In Tuscany, chefs fill every kind of vegetable; try small squash, mushrooms, even artichokes!

Vegetables

10   5-inch-long zucchini
½   teaspoon coarse salt
5   long mildly hot red peppers
10   tigerella tomatoes or any
     medium red or yellow tomatoes

Filling

3   tablespoons extra-virgin
    olive oil, plus enough to drizzle
2   garlic cloves, sliced very thin
¾   pound lean ground pork
    Salt and freshly ground pepper
¼   teaspoon sugar
1   pinch red hot pepper flakes
2   medium onions, finely chopped
6   cremini mushrooms, finely
    chopped
1   tablespoon chopped fresh sage

To prepare the vegetables for stuffing, slice the zucchini in half lengthwise. Using a melon baller, scoop out the core and seeds. Sprinkle the zucchini with ½ teaspoon salt and allow to sit 30 minutes upside down on a dish towel. Rinse in cold water and pat dry. Slice the red peppers in half lengthwise and seed them. Cut off the tops of the tomatoes and gently scoop out the seeds with a sharp spoon.

opposite: *I arranged the buffet items on pale green and aqua Colorstax platters. Made by the California pottery Metlox, these dishes come in lovely muted or bright colors, and they're great for entertaining. Everything was crowded onto the pine country serving table—the array was tempting and delectable.*

To make the filling, preheat the oven to 375° F. In a large skillet heat 1 tablespoon of the olive oil over medium heat. Stir in the garlic and sauté for 3 minutes. Add the ground pork, ¼ teaspoon salt, and the sugar. Increase the heat to high and sauté for 5 minutes to brown the meat, adding the red pepper flakes and black pepper to taste.

In a separate skillet, heat the remaining 2 tablespoons of olive oil over medium heat and sauté the onions and mushrooms for 5 minutes until soft. Add to the browned pork mixture and combine well. Spoon the filling into the prepared vegetables.

Line roasting pans or heavy baking sheets with parchment paper and place the filled vegetables in them. Drizzle the vegetables with additional olive oil and sprinkle with sage, salt, and pepper. Bake until tender, about 20 minutes.

Roasted
TOMATOES
Topped with
WHITE BEANS

Serves 20

Two simple ingredients—tomatoes and white beans—are easily transformed into a mouthwatering dish that always evokes Tuscany for me.

½   pound dried white beans,
    picked over
3   tablespoons extra-virgin olive oil
2   garlic cloves, sliced thin
2½   teaspoons coarse salt
½   cup fresh coriander leaves,
    chopped
2½   teaspoons freshly ground black
    pepper
3   large beefsteak tomatoes, cut
    into 1-inch thick slices
1   tablespoon sugar

In a saucepan cover the beans with cold water. Bring to a boil over medium-high heat, then reduce to low and cook for 1 hour until soft. Drain.

Preheat the oven to 400° F.

Heat the olive oil in a pan, add the garlic, and sauté for 2 minutes. Add the beans, ½ teaspoon of the salt, the coriander, and ½ teaspoon of the black pepper and toss quickly to mix. Remove from the heat.

Line a baking sheet with parchment paper. Arrange the tomato slices on the sheet and sprinkle with 2 teaspoons of the salt, 2 teaspoons of the pepper, and the sugar. Roast for 15 to 20 minutes. The tomatoes will deepen in color and become somewhat dry.

Transfer to a serving platter. Place a tablespoon of white beans in the center of each slice and serve either warm or cold.

right: *Burpee's 'North Star' hybrid peppers can be picked while still green, but they also mature early to a bright red. With firm, sweet flesh, they have three to four lobes, making them good "stuffers." These red peppers and some green 'Big Dippers' were filled with my friend Necy's rice and baked with the tops replaced over the filling.*

left: *Burpee's 'Great Stuff' peppers are sweet and large, with firm walls; they're also very good for stuffing. Six to 8 inches long, they ripen first to green and later to dark red. I cut them in half lengthwise and filled them with a fragrant stuffing made from Basmati rice, capers, raisins, and cilantro.*

Roasted PEPPERS with a VARIETY OF FILLINGS

Serves 20

Any one of these delicious fillings can be used as a side dish to accompany meat or fish, but they are especially nice used as fillings for peppers, whether green or red, yellow or orange.

Prepare the peppers by cutting off their stem ends. Reserve the tops. Remove the seeds and membrane. Or you can cut the peppers in half lengthwise and remove the seeds and membrane.

Once the peppers are filled, preheat the oven to 375° F. Arrange the peppers upright on baking sheets, replace the tops if desired, and roast for 25 to 40 minutes, depending on size.

Couscous Filling

Makes enough for 3 to 5 peppers

¾ cup dried currants
½ cup plus ⅓ cup fresh orange juice
3 tablespoons unsalted butter
1 large red onion, quartered and sliced
2 cups chicken stock
2 cups couscous
2 teaspoons fresh rosemary, chopped
½ teaspoon freshly ground nutmeg
Salt and freshly ground pepper

Plump the currants in ½ cup of the orange juice for 15 minutes. In a large saucepan, melt 1 tablespoon of the butter over medium-high heat. Add the onion and sauté for 5 minutes, until soft. Add ⅓ cup of the orange juice and the chicken stock. Raise the heat to high and bring to a boil. Sprinkle the couscous into the liquid, stirring constantly.

Cover the pan, reduce the heat to medium, and cook the couscous for 15 to 20 minutes, stirring occasionally so the couscous does not stick. Remove the pan from the heat and stir in the remaining 2 tablespoons of butter.

Add the currants with their juice, rosemary, and nutmeg. Season with salt and pepper. Fill the prepared peppers with the couscous mixture and roast as above.

Basmati Rice Filling

Makes enough for 3 peppers

2½ cups water
1 cup Basmati rice
3 tablespoons unsalted butter
1 medium onion, finely chopped
2 garlic cloves, finely chopped
2 tablespoons capers
½ cup golden raisins
½ cup unsalted pistachio nuts, chopped coarsely
½ cup fresh cilantro leaves, chopped
Salt and freshly ground pepper

In a saucepan, bring the water to a boil over high heat. Add the Basmati rice, cover the pan tightly, and reduce the heat to a simmer. Simmer the rice for 25 minutes. Drain well.

Meanwhile, in a large skillet, melt the butter over medium-high heat. Add the onion and sauté for 5 minutes, until soft. Add the garlic and sauté for 1 more minute. Stir in, one ingredient at a time, the capers, golden raisins, pistachios, and cilantro, sautéing each ingredient for 1 minute. Add the cooked Basmati rice and remove the skillet from the heat. Season with salt and pepper. Fill the prepared peppers with the rice mixture and roast as above.

Necy's Rice Filling

Makes enough for 10 peppers

4 tablespoons vegetable oil
2 cups uncooked white rice
½ small green cabbage, cut into large shreds
1 red bell pepper, seeded and chopped
1 yellow bell pepper, seeded and chopped
2 medium onions, quartered
1 teaspoon fresh thyme leaves, chopped
1 teaspoon fresh parsley, chopped
Salt and freshly ground pepper
4 cups boiling water

In a large, shallow pan, heat the vegetable oil over medium-high heat. Add the rice and sauté for 6 minutes, stirring constantly.

Add the cabbage, peppers, onions, thyme, parsley, and salt and pepper. Sauté with the rice for 3 minutes longer.

Reduce the heat to low, add the boiling water, and cover the pan. Simmer the rice for 20 to 30 minutes until tender, stirring once or twice and adding a bit more water if necessary.

Fill the prepared peppers with the rice mixture and roast as above.

Orzo and Portobello Mushroom Filling

Makes enough for 3 large peppers

1 cup orzo
½ pound portobello mushrooms, washed and roughly chopped
2 tablespoons extra-virgin olive oil
1 cup dry white wine
1 bunch arugula, washed, stemmed, and roughly chopped
½ cup grated Parmesan cheese
1 teaspoon coarse salt
1 teaspoon freshly ground pepper

In a large stockpot, cook the orzo in boiling water for 15 to 20 minutes, until al dente. Drain.

In a large skillet, sauté the mushrooms in the olive oil over medium-high heat for 5 minutes. Add the wine and arugula and cook for 1 minute. Remove the skillet from the heat and stir in the orzo and Parmesan cheese. Season with salt and pepper. Fill the prepared peppers with the orzo mixture and roast as above.

Grilled CIPOLLA ONIONS *in Balsamic* VINEGAR SAUCE

Serves 20

Cipolla onions are a flat, small, dense variety that can be found year-round in gourmet green grocers. They are fragrant and tender and have a sweet flesh.

1 pound cipolla onions, peeled, stem point intact
1½ tablespoons balsamic vinegar

I used extra old grange chairs as side tables for flowers and drinks.

1½ tablespoons extra-virgin olive oil
12 sage leaves, cut into strips
2 tablespoons fresh rosemary leaves, chopped
1 teaspoon fresh thyme leaves, chopped
1 teaspoon fresh marjoram leaves, chopped
Salt and freshly ground pepper

Fill a pot with water, add the onions, and bring to a boil. Reduce the heat and simmer for 5 minutes. Drain the onions.

Using a cast-iron grill pan, grill the onions over medium-high heat about 5 minutes per side, until just tender and browned.

In a large bowl whisk together the vinegar, olive oil, sage, rosemary, thyme, marjoram, and salt and pepper to taste.

Toss the grilled onions in the marinade and allow to marinate at least 1 to 2 hours before serving.

Stuffed ROLY-POLY ZUCCHINI

Serves 20

Roly-Poly zucchini are a relatively new introduction to the market. They are tender and when cooked do not get wet and mushy. Sliced, topped with Parmesan and bread crumbs, and toasted, they are delicious.

3 Roly-Poly zucchini
2 cups bread crumbs
¾ cup grated Parmesan cheese
3 tablespoons unsalted butter, melted
1 tablespoon fresh oregano leaves, chopped
1 tablespoon fresh parsley, chopped
Salt and freshly ground pepper
Lemon wedges

Preheat the oven to 350° F. Line a baking sheet with parchment paper.

Cut the zucchini into 1½-inch-thick slices, discarding the ends. Using a melon baller, scoop out a 2-inch circle in the center of each slice about ½-inch deep.

Fill a large stockpot ¾ full of water and bring to a boil over high heat. Immerse the zucchini slices and blanch for 2 minutes. Drain and pat dry.

Place the slices hollowed side up on the baking sheet. In a medium bowl, mix the bread crumbs, Parmesan cheese, butter, oregano, and parsley. Fill the hollowed circles of the zucchini with the mixture. Toast in the oven for 5 minutes until lightly browned. Sprinkle very lightly with salt and pepper and serve with lemon wedges.

above: *I first tasted cipolla onions in Viareggio in a seaside restaurant famous for its country fare. When grilled in balsamic vinegar and marinated with herbs, they take on a unique sweet flavor, unlike any other onion. The serving dish is Syracuse China, a very collectible pottery.*

Wine-Poached
SUMMER FRUITS

Serves 20

A buffet is all about abundance and sampling. Poach many fruits—they'll all disappear. Use only unblemished fruits, and smell them for fragrance to check for ripeness. If there is little or no perfume, don't buy them!

Apricots, Golden Figs, and 'Donut' Peaches in White Wine

2–3 sprigs sweet woodruff
1 bottle Riesling wine
½ cup sugar
1 fresh vanilla bean, split lengthwise
10 ripe, firm 'Donut' peaches
10 ripe, firm apricots
10 ripe, firm golden figs
1 cup crème fraîche (page 40)
Sprigs of mint, lemon balm, or spearmint for garnish

Insert two or three small sprigs of sweet woodruff into a bottle of Riesling wine. Replace the cork and refrigerate for 2 weeks.

Wash the fruit. To poach, in a large pot combine the wine, sugar, and vanilla bean. Bring to a boil over high heat. Reduce the heat to a simmer, add the peaches, and simmer for 5 to 10 minutes, until tender but not soft. Remove the peaches with a slotted spoon to a dish.

Add the apricots to the wine and simmer for 5 to 10 minutes, until tender but not soft. Remove the apricots to a separate plate. Add the figs to the wine and simmer for 10 to 15 minutes. Remove the figs to their own dish.

Raise heat to medium high and cook the poaching liquid to reduce it by two-thirds, about 20 minutes. To serve, arrange a selection of fruit on individual plates. Drizzle with a spoonful of poaching liquid. Garnish with crème fraîche and sprigs of mint, lemon balm, or spearmint.

Yellow Peaches, Plums, Nectarines, and Black Figs in Red Wine

10 ripe, firm yellow peaches
5 ripe, firm plums
5 ripe, firm nectarines
5 ripe, firm black figs
1 bottle dry red wine
½ cup sugar
2 star anise
2 black peppercorns
1 cup crème fraîche (page 40)
Sprigs of fresh mint, lemon balm, or spearmint for garnish

Wash the fruit. In a large pot, combine the wine, sugar, star anise, and peppercorns, and bring to a boil. Reduce the heat to a simmer, add the peaches, and simmer for 5 to 10 minutes, until tender but not soft. Remove the peaches with a slotted spoon to a plate.

Add the plums to the wine and simmer for 5 to 10 minutes, until tender but not soft. Remove the plums to a separate plate.

Add the nectarines to the wine and simmer for 5 to 10 minutes, until tender but not soft. Remove the nectarines to a separate dish. Add the figs to the wine, simmer for 10 to 15 minutes, then remove them to their own plate.

Raise the heat to medium high and cook the poaching liquid to reduce it by two-thirds, about 20 minutes.

To serve, arrange the fruit on individual plates. Drizzle with a spoonful of poaching liquid. Garnish with crème fraîche and sprigs of mint, lemon balm, or spearmint.

opposite: *Garnished with dollops of crème fraîche, an assortment of wine-poached fruits—figs, plums, nectarines, and peaches—was lovely.* **above:** *Summertime, of course, is the best time to cook with local fruits and vegetables, when they are plentiful, inexpensive, and most flavorful. I search the local farmstands and orchards for the best of the best: ripe, perfumed apricots and sweet, juicy nectarines. The plate is Sterling vitrified china, made for diner use in East Liverpool, Ohio.* **below:** *Green and black figs are available in markets at the same time. These small, firm figs grow wonderfully in warmer climes and are excellent when poached.*

10

the best **Clambake**

Serves 30

Steamed *Clam* Sacks with *Sausage, Corn,* and Red *Potato*

✳ Roasted *Vegetable* Sandwiches

Lobsters Steamed over Seaweed

Herb-Garlic Bread ✳ Spicy Salt-Rubbed *Chicken*

✳ Little *Fruit* Pies

Lexi's Favorite *Chocolate Chip* Cookies

the best Clambake

IT TAKES A LOT OF PLANNING, AND A LOT OF LUGGING, BUT A REAL PIT-DUG CLAMBAKE IS PERHAPS ONE OF THE MOST ENJOYABLE WAYS TO ENTERTAIN A LARGE GROUP OF FRIENDS. LAST YEAR WITH MY MAGAZINE STAFF I INSTITUTED THE *MARTHA STEWART LIVING* ANNUAL CLAMBAKE ON THE BEACH NEAREST MY HOME IN EAST HAMPTON, LONG ISLAND. THE TOWN PERMITS CLAMBAKES IF ALL EVIDENCE IS GONE WHEN YOU LEAVE THE BEACH. I BROUGHT HICKORY WOOD FROM CONNECTI-CUT TO BURN IN THE GIANT PITS WE DUG ON THE BEACH. SMALL CHEESECLOTH SACKS WERE FILLED WITH AN EAR OF CORN, A SAUSAGE, A POTATO OR TWO, AND LITTLENECK CLAMS AND THEN COVERED IN SEAWEED AND STEAMED IN GIANT GALVANIZED STEEL TUBS THAT I HAD BOUGHT FROM MY LOCAL HARDWARE STORE. LOBSTERS STEAMED SEPARATELY, ALSO UNDER A THICK COVER OF SEAWEED. GARLIC BREAD WAS GRILLED ON THE BIG GRILLS WE TOTED TO THE BEACH, ALONG WITH THE SPICY SALT-RUBBED CHICKEN. AND FOR DESSERT WE HAD COOKIES AND HEAVENLY LITTLE FRUIT-FILLED PIES OF BLUEBERRY, PEACH, APRICOT, AND PLUM IN FLAKY OLD-FASHIONED CRUSTS. THE ONLY PROBLEM: WHICH PIE TO CHOOSE? BESIDES MY MAGAZINE STAFF, MANY FRIENDS DROPPED BY, SOME WITH CHILDREN, WHEN THEY GOT WORD, OR WHIFF, OF THE GOINGS-ON AT THE BEACH!

previous page: *The cheesecloth sacks contained clams, sausage, corn, and red potatoes. We made one for each of the guests—as well as a dozen extras for unexpected drop-ins.*

left: *I bought 50 one-pound lobsters, a very economical way to purchase these usually expensive crustaceans.*

below left: *The thickly sliced onions were marinated in olive oil and then grilled over hot charcoal.*

below right: *Despite gusty winds and even a sprinkling of rain, my young friends Monica Pasternak, Monica Mendez, and Oana Teleman enjoyed the clambake thoroughly!*

first: Great big steel tubs were perfect for our New England–style clambake. While we were at Georgica Pond, Renato and Renaldo were busy digging the giant pits for the fires.

second: To make the sacks, cut the cheesecloth into sixteen-inch squares and tie the little bundles with kitchen twine. It's a good idea to use a double thickness of the cheesecloth for extra strength.

third: Always rinse the lobsters and the seaweed thoroughly before layering them in the tub. Make sure the bottom layer of seaweed is especially thick, since this will be the hottest part.

fourth: Louise prepared some of the galvanized tubs; she layered lots of seaweed with cheesecloth packets or lobsters, and waited until the hickory wood logs had burned down to smoldering red-hot coals.

fifth: The pits were full of perfect hot coals when the tubs of lobsters and the cheesecloth packets were placed within, atop supports made of rabbit wire. The lobsters steamed to doneness within 35 to 40 minutes. Be sure to check; don't overcook.

sixth: The steamed clam sacks cooked more quickly than the lobsters. Monica, the six-year-old daughter of my friend Marie Mendez, loved the sweet corn, even if her teeth were loose.

seventh: We used striped cotton tablecloths and napkins, with bright blue enamelware. At the end of the party, everything was carried back to my house in the tubs—the trash, the coals, the recyclables. Then the tubs were scrubbed clean and put away for the next annual clambake!

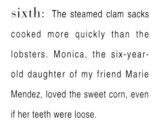

Steamed CLAM SACKS *with* SAUSAGE, CORN, *and* RED POTATO

Serves 30

These little sacks are steamed to perfection in the pits.

30 sausages, preferably fresh chorizos
 1 bushel littleneck clams
     Cotton cheesecloth
30 small red new potatoes, scrubbed
30 ears of corn, shucked
     Cotton kitchen string
     Cayenne-Lime Butter
     (recipe follows)
     Salt and freshly ground pepper

At home, lightly brown the sausages in a skillet over medium-high heat for 3 to 5 minutes and drain on paper towels. Reserve, covered, in the refrigerator for up to 12 hours before the clambake.

Scrub and rinse the clams well and keep them in ice until ready to cook.

Cut the cheesecloth into 30 16-inch squares of double thickness. Wrap up 2 clams, 1 sausage, 1 potato, and 1 ear of corn in each. Bring the corners of the cheesecloth together and tightly tie the sacks with kitchen string. Steam the sacks buried in seaweed in the galvanized tubs for 10 to 15 minutes, or until the clam shells open. Serve with Cayenne-Lime Butter, salt, and pepper.

above: *While I supervised the canoe races, Zacki acted as barbecue chef, tending to the salt-rubbed chickens that grilled slowly, without burning, over hot charcoal fires. The grill was made especially for me by an Argentinian polo player who is also an excellent welder and metal fabricator.*

Clambake

Cayenne-Lime Butter

Makes 4 cups

4 cups (8 sticks) unsalted butter
1 tablespoon cayenne pepper
Juice of 3 limes

In a saucepan, melt the butter with the cayenne and lime juice. Serve in small bowls.

Roasted VEGETABLE SANDWICHES

Serves 30

Flavored with basil and thyme, vegetables and sweet onions are excellent as sandwich filling.

12 red bell peppers
14 large sweet onions, thickly sliced (I use Vidalias)
3 large eggplants, sliced in rounds
   Extra-virgin olive oil
1 cup thyme leaves, finely chopped
30 large seven-grain buns, split
   Mayonnaise
2 cups basil leaves, chopped
   Salt and freshly ground pepper

Grill the bell peppers on the charcoal grill until tender and charred; when cool, peel, seed, and slice.

Grill the onion and eggplant slices on the charcoal grill, 3 to 5 minutes per side, until tender and charred. Brush with olive oil and sprinkle with thyme while grilling.

The buns can be toasted, split, on the grill if you like. Spread both sides lightly with mayonnaise and layer with either basil, onion, roasted pepper, and salt and pepper, or eggplant, onion, roasted pepper, and salt and pepper.

LOBSTERS Steamed over Seaweed

Serves 30

Using one-pound lobsters really cuts down the cooking time, so be sure not to overcook. You will need two large, wide galvanized steel tubs to cook the lobsters and clam sacks.

2 bushels fresh seaweed, washed
30 1-pound lobsters
4 cups (8 sticks) unsalted butter, melted

Cover the bottom of the tubs with a thick layer of seaweed.

Layer some of the lobsters in the seaweed, making sure they are well covered.

Steam for 20 to 30 minutes until the lobsters turn bright red, then remove. Continue adding lobsters as others finish cooking.

To serve, crack the claws with a nut cracker or use a rubber mallet and bread board. Split the tail and body to make it easier to extract the lobster meat. Serve hot with melted butter.

Herb-Garlic BREAD

Serves 30

You cannot make enough of this bread!

8 garlic cloves, minced
½ cup chopped parsley, chervil, and thyme, mixed
1½ cups (3 sticks) unsalted butter, melted
6 loaves Italian bread, sliced thickly to within ½ inch of bottom of loaf

Combine the garlic and herbs with the melted butter in a small bowl. Brush the butter between the slices of each loaf. Wrap each loaf in aluminum foil and toast on the grill for 5 minutes, turning to ensure even toasting.

SPICY Salt-Rubbed CHICKEN

Serves 30

The marinade and fresh herbs in this recipe make the chicken juicy and flavorful.

15 chickens, cut in quarters
1 cup fresh lemon juice
2 cups extra-virgin olive oil
1 cup oregano leaves, finely chopped
1 cup rosemary leaves, finely chopped
1 cup thyme leaves, finely chopped
1 cup coarse salt
½ cup freshly ground pepper

Wash the chicken pieces in cold water and pat dry with paper towels.

Whisk together the lemon juice and olive oil in a very large bowl. Add the chicken and marinate, refrigerated, for 1 hour.

Combine the oregano, rosemary, thyme, salt, and pepper in a big bowl. Dredge each piece of chicken in the mixture to evenly coat.

Grill the chicken over medium coals for 20 to 25 minutes, turning halfway through the cooking time, until the juice of the chicken runs clear when pierced with a knife.

Clambake

Little
FRUIT PIES

Makes 30 pies

Many fruits can be used to make delectable pies. Season plums with mace, apricots with nutmeg, and peaches with cinnamon. Blueberries should have no spice added.

Country Pie Pastry
(recipe follows)
2 quarts blueberries
2 pounds each peaches, apricots, plums, peeled, pitted, and sliced
2 cups sugar
2 cups (4 sticks) unsalted butter
   Cinnamon
   Nutmeg
   Mace
1 cup heavy cream
3 large egg yolks, lightly beaten

Preheat the oven to 375° F.

Roll out the pie pastry on a lightly floured board. Using a sharp knife, cut out 30 six-inch circles of pie crust. Place the crusts into 30 four-inch individual tins, allowing excess pastry to hang over the rim.

Fill each pie with ½ cup fruit. Sprinkle each with 1 tablespoon sugar and dot with 1 tablespoon butter. Season with a pinch of cinnamon, nutmeg, or mace, depending on the fruit. Bring up the edges of the pie dough and fold over the fruit in a rustic fashion. Right before baking, combine the heavy cream and egg yolks in a mixing bowl and brush the pastry with the mixture. This causes the pastry to brown richly.

Place the individual pies spaced ½ inch apart on large baking sheets and bake for 35 to 40 minutes until the crusts are golden brown. Transfer the pies to a cooling rack until cooled to room temperature. Serve in pie tins.

Country Pie
Pastry

*Makes enough for
30 little pies*

4½ cups all-purpose flour
1 teaspoon salt
¼ cup sugar
1½ cups (3 sticks) unsalted butter, chilled and cut into pieces
½ cup vegetable shortening
⅓ to ½ cup ice-cold water

In a food processor, add the flour, salt, sugar, butter, and shortening. Pulse for 30 seconds until the mixture resembles coarse meal. Add ice-cold water, 1 tablespoon at a time, until the dough just holds together.

Divide the dough into thirds and shape into flat round discs. Wrap in plastic and chill for 1 hour in the refrigerator.

Lexi's Favorite
CHOCOLATE CHIP
COOKIES

*Makes 30
4-inch cookies*

Actually, these are everyone's favorite chocolate chip cookies!

2 cups (4 sticks) unsalted butter, softened
3 cups brown sugar
1 cup sugar
4 large eggs
2 teaspoons vanilla extract
3½ cups all-purpose flour
1½ teaspoons salt
2 teaspoons baking soda
1½ cups semisweet chocolate chips

Preheat the oven to 375° F. Line baking sheets with parchment paper.

Cream the butter in a large bowl until smooth; add the brown and granulated sugars. Beat in the eggs and vanilla until well blended.

In another large bowl, sift together the flour, salt, and baking soda. Beat this into the butter mixture. Stir in the chocolate chips.

Drop 2 to 3 tablespoons of batter onto the baking sheet, 2 inches apart. Bake for 8 minutes until golden brown.

Remove the cookies from the baking sheet and cool on a rack.

The day before the clambake, I made pies in recyclable aluminum "tins" and used an old-fashioned single-crust method for the pastry to avoid rolling out two pieces of dough per pie. Just fold up the edges of the bottom crust to encase the filling. Don't forget to season each pie with a spice that is complementary to the fruit.

11

Surprisingly SIMPLE Chinese

Serves 10

Boiled *Peanuts* with Star Anise　✳　*Lotus Root* with Red Pepper

Chinese *Spinach*　✳　*Bitter* Melon with *Baby Shrimp*

Bean Curd with Pickled Cabbage　✳　Chinese *Egg* Whites with *Tomatoes*

Pork with *Mushrooms* and Water Chestnuts　✳　Hunan-Style Steamed *Black* Sea Bass

Chinese Fried Fish　✳　*Shrimp* with Ginger and Scallion

Chopped Tender *Mustard* Greens　✳　Sweet *Sausage* with Green Beans

Spinach Stems with *Black Beans*　✳　Rice with Chinese Sausage and Smoked Pork

Rice Soup with *Coriander* Leaves　✳　Pickled *Ginger*

Lichees on Ice

Surprisingly SIMPLE Chinese

WHEN I WAS A CHILD, MY FATHER WOULD TAKE ME TO NEW YORK'S CHINATOWN ONCE OR TWICE A YEAR. THERE WE WOULD EXPLORE THE MARKETS AND ENJOY A MEMORABLE LUNCH AT A CHINESE RESTAURANT. HIS METHOD FOR CHOOSING A PLACE WAS SIMPLE: PICK A RESTAURANT WHERE ONLY CHINESE PEOPLE WERE DINING. IT WORKED, AND WE ORDERED NOT FROM THE INCOMPREHENSIBLE MENU, BUT FROM OUR NEIGHBORS' PLATES, USING SIGN LANGUAGE AND POINTING. WE ALWAYS ENDED UP WITH UNUSUAL DELICACIES, AND THE BILL, WHEN IT CAME, WAS ALWAYS WITHIN OUR MEAGER BUDGET. I FELT PRIVILEGED TO SHARE A MEAL WITH MY FATHER IN AN EXOTIC ATMOSPHERE, AND HIS WILLINGNESS TO EXPERIMENT WAS PASSED ON TO ME. OVER THE YEARS I HAVE KEPT LISTS OF THE CHINESE DISHES I ESPECIALLY LIKE, AND A CHINESE FRIEND, LILY PEI, HAS SHARED SOME OF HER RECIPES WITH ME. THE SECRET OF A GOOD HOME-COOKED CHINESE MEAL IS TOTAL ORGANIZATION: ALL INGREDIENTS MUST BE "PREPPED" BEFORE COOKING. I PREPARE A TRAY FOR EACH DISH, WITH MANY SMALL BOWLS TO HOLD THE INGREDIENTS. SAUCES ARE PREMEASURED AND ALL SPICES ARE COLLECTED ON THE TRAY. GUESTS ARE INVITED TO SIT DOWN AND I COOK TWO OR THREE DISHES AT A TIME. AFTER WE HAVE SAMPLED THESE, I COOK SOME MORE. AND THEN A BIT MORE!

previous page: *I discov-
ered lichees as a child when my
dad brought these small prickly
brownish red fruits home in
paper bags. I often like to serve
them on a bowl of ice cubes,
peeled, for guests to enjoy at the
end of the meal.*

above: *Portion plates in a
green Blue Willow pattern
served as the large plates. The
fine rice soup was offered in
inexpensive celadon bowls. Both
the fried and the steamed sea
bass were served whole. My
trees were full of fruit, so these
were my centerpiece.*

above: A good snack food, boiled peanuts are both tasty and nutritious. They are easily cooked and then, piled in bowls for guests to shell and eat, they are devoured like popcorn. right: Lotus root is another unusual Chinese vegetable, one that is simple to prepare. Sliced thin and cooked with vinegar and sugar, this hard vegetable becomes tender and delicious in a matter of minutes.

left: Chinese spinach is very similar to leafy American-style spinach. Cooked in a wok with garlic, olive oil, salt, and water, the leaves become tender and soft. right: Shrimp with ginger and scallion is easy to prepare and very tasty. bottom: Bitter melon is like a bumpy cucumber; squeeze it before cooking to remove excess moisture.

I purchased my first wok in Chinatown many years ago. I still have it, and take care of it as I was taught to by a chef at one of my favorite restaurants, Joy Luck, in Chinatown. Never use soap in a wok; always wash it while still hot from the stove with very hot water; use a bamboo brush to scrub; and dry over a low flame to prevent rusting.

Boiled PEANUTS with STAR ANISE

Serves 10

Raw peanuts are available in specialty markets and in Chinese neighborhoods. Serve this wonderful appetizer with ice-cold Chinese beer or hot fragrant green tea.

4 cups water
1 pound fresh raw peanuts in the shell
2 star anise
2 teaspoons coarse salt

In a large saucepan bring the water to a boil. Add the peanuts, star anise, and salt. Simmer for 20 minutes, then drain the peanuts. When they have cooled, serve them in the shell to be peeled at the table.

LOTUS ROOT with Red Pepper

Serves 10

Buy lotus root that is very fresh; when peeled it should be white and unblemished.

1½ pounds fresh lotus root
1 tablespoon lemon juice
2 tablespoons sugar
2 tablespoons Chinese grain vinegar
1 tablespoon extra-virgin olive oil
1 teaspoon coarse salt
½ hot red pepper, chopped

Wash the lotus root and peel with a vegetable peeler. Cut it crosswise into ⅛-inch-thick rounds. Keep the rounds from discoloring by soaking them in cold water with the lemon juice.

In a small bowl, mix together the sugar and grain vinegar.

Heat a wok over high heat, then add the oil.

While the oil is heating, drain the lotus root and pat it dry. When the oil is hot, add the lotus, lower the heat to medium, and quickly stir-fry. Add the sugar and vinegar mixture in 4 parts, allowing each addition to evaporate before adding the next.

In the last 30 seconds sprinkle the lotus root with salt, then remove from the heat. The entire cooking time should be about 5 to 6 minutes. Garnish with the chopped pepper and serve immediately.

Chinese SPINACH

Serves 10

The flavor of this spinach is enhanced by the steaming process—be sure to let the moisture all but evaporate before serving.

1½ pounds Chinese spinach, leaves only
1½ tablespoons extra-virgin olive oil
2 garlic cloves, sliced thin
1 cup cold water
1 teaspoon coarse salt

Wash the Chinese spinach well. Remove the stems and spin the leaves dry. Heat a wok over high heat, then add the oil. When the oil is hot add the garlic, using a wok utensil to stir it quickly. Do not allow it to burn. Add the Chinese spinach and quickly stir-fry until it wilts down to the rim of the wok.

Add the cold water and sprinkle the salt over the spinach. Lower the heat to medium-high, cover the wok, and allow the spinach to steam for 5 minutes, without stirring. Remove the lid and toss the spinach, allowing moisture to evaporate. Remove from the heat and serve immediately.

BITTER MELON with BABY SHRIMP

Serves 10

This delicious dish takes only 4 minutes to stir-fry.

1 pound Chinese bitter melon
1 tablespoon coarse salt, plus more for seasoning
½ cup dried baby shrimp
1 tablespoon extra-virgin olive oil

To prepare the melon, slice it in half lengthwise and clean out the seeds with a spoon. Remove the rind and slice the melon thinly crosswise.

Place the sliced melon in a medium bowl, sprinkle with 1 tablespoon salt, and toss lightly. Allow it to rest in the bowl for 1 hour. Drain off the liquid and squeeze any excess moisture from the slices with your fingers.

Rinse the dried shrimp with water and drain well.

Heat a wok over high heat, then add the oil. When the oil is hot, stir in the dried shrimp and toss for 30 seconds. Add the melon slices and stir-fry for 2 minutes.

Sprinkle salt to taste over the mixture and stir-fry for 1 minute longer. Serve immediately.

Note: To stir-fry, use a special Chinese long-handled spoon. Stir the contents of the wok by lifting and turning the ingredients to cook everything evenly. Remember, what cooks fastest are those ingredients touching the steel, so constant turning or "stir-frying" is essential. Having sufficient liquid is also essential. I have substituted water for oil to cut down on fat in these recipes. This may change the recipe from the original Chinese, but the dishes are still wonderfully flavorful.

left and below: *The more you examine the cuisine of China, the more you realize how very thorough and basic it is. This simple dish of tomatoes and egg whites is typically uncomplicated but full of flavor.*

above: *Placing all the ingredients for a recipe in small dishes like these makes the organization of this menu much easier. It would be impossible to proceed with the many dishes in the meal unless everything was chopped and measured in advance.*

above: *The stir-fried bean curd is made special with the addition of salty Szechuan pickled cabbage. The chives with flower buds add to the dish as well.* left: *The celadon dishes I used for this meal were made in Japan, China, and England. The sterling silver chopsticks and fish rest were made in China.*

BEAN CURD *with* *Pickled* CABBAGE

Serves 10

Salty pickled cabbage is a staple of Szechuan cooking. It can be found in Chinese markets and can be kept refrigerated for a long time.

- 2 squares (½ pound) firm bean curd
- 1 bunch chives, with flowers if possible
- 3 tablespoons vegetable oil
- ½ cup pickled cabbage
- 1 red bell pepper, seeded and chopped
- ¼ teaspoon coarse salt
- 1 tablespoon light soy sauce
- 1 teaspoon sesame oil

Cut each bean curd into 1-inch squares. Cut chives into 2-inch lengths, keeping the flowers.

Heat a wok over high heat, then add the vegetable oil. When the oil is hot, add the bean curd and sauté for 1 minute. Add the pickled cabbage and the red pepper. Sauté for 1 minute, then move the mixture to one side of the wok.

Quickly add the chives and the salt, and tilt the wok toward the chives. This allows you to sauté the chives briefly (about 1 minute), without overcooking the red pepper and pickled cabbage. Combine the cabbage and peppers with the chives.

Add the soy sauce and sauté for 1 minute longer, then add the sesame oil and immediately remove the mixture from the heat to a serving plate.

Chinese EGG WHITES *with* TOMATOES

Serves 10

Chinese cooking is like magic: with just 2 tomatoes and 10 egg whites, a delicious dish is created.

- 2 tablespoons plus ½ teaspoon vegetable oil
- 2 large tomatoes, sliced
- 10 large egg whites
- 1½ teaspoons coarse salt
- ¼ teaspoon white pepper

Heat a wok over high heat, then add ½ teaspoon of the oil. When the oil is hot, add the tomato slices. Quickly stir for 1 minute. Immediately remove the tomato slices to a plate and set aside. Wash the wok thoroughly.

In a medium bowl, whisk the egg whites with 1 teaspoon of salt until foamy.

Return the wok to high heat and add the remaining 2 tablespoons of oil. When the oil is hot, scoop up some of it using a wok utensil; hold this oil over the wok. With your free hand, pour the egg whites into the wok and immediately pour the hot oil directly over the egg whites. Cook for 1 minute. When puffed, add the cooked tomato slices and stir quickly. Add the remaining salt and white pepper. Serve hot.

PORK *with* MUSHROOMS *and* *Water Chestnuts*

Serves 10

Use dried or fresh wood ear mushrooms to add an unusual flavor and texture.

- ¼ cup dried wood ear mushrooms, or ¼ pound fresh
- ½ pound lean pork fillet
- 1 pound fresh or canned water chestnuts, sliced
- ½ teaspoon cornstarch
- 1 tablespoon light soy sauce
- 2 tablespoons extra-virgin olive oil
- 1 teaspoon coarse salt
- 1 scallion, chopped

Soak the dried wood ear mushrooms for several hours or overnight in cold water to rehydrate them. Chill the pork fillet almost to freezing to make slicing easier.

If using fresh water chestnuts, wash them thoroughly in cold water. Peel them using a paring knife to remove just the brown skin. Slice them thinly into ⅛-inch rounds.

Slice the pork fillet, then cut slices into thin strips. In a medium bowl mix together the cornstarch and light soy sauce. Add the pork strips and toss until they are completely coated. Drain the mushrooms well.

Heat a wok over high heat, then add 1 tablespoon of the oil. When the oil is hot add the mushrooms and ½ teaspoon of the salt. Stir-fry for 1 minute, then transfer the mushrooms to a bowl. Wash the wok, and reheat. When hot, add the remaining oil. When the oil is hot, add the scallion and water chestnuts, stirring constantly for 1 minute. Add the pork and sauté for 1 to 2 minutes, until the pork loses its pink color.

Add the mushrooms and stir-fry for 30 seconds. Remove from the heat and serve immediately.

Hunan-Style STEAMED BLACK SEA BASS

Serves 10

I love fermented black beans, and they impart a unique flavor to this simple fish.

1 2-pound black sea bass, cleaned and scaled, head and tail on
2 ½-inch slices fresh ginger
3 scallions
1 tablespoon coarse salt
2 tablespoons fermented black beans
1 teaspoon extra-virgin olive oil
½ tablespoon Chinese black vinegar
2 tablespoons shredded fresh ginger

Rub the black sea bass inside and out with a piece of ginger. Fill the cavity with the 2 pieces of ginger and 1 whole scallion. Place the fish into a ceramic baking dish that is just large enough to hold the fish yet able to fit into a wok. Sprinkle the salt over the fish, wrap with plastic wrap, and refrigerate until ready to cook. Julienne the remaining 2 scallions into 1-inch lengths.

Place a rack in the bottom of a wok. Pour in 4 cups of water and bring to a boil. When the water boils, place the baking dish with the fish on the rack. Sprinkle the fermented black beans over the fish, cover the wok, and allow the fish to steam for 10 minutes.

Remove the dish and the rack from the wok, pour out the water, and dry the wok completely. Return the wok to the burner.

Remove the ginger and scallion from the cavity of the fish and discard; reserve the cooking juices. Place the fish on a serving dish.

Heat the wok over high heat, then add the oil. When the oil is hot, add the black vinegar, shredded ginger, julienned scallions, and the reserved cooking juices. Toss for 30 seconds, remove from the heat, and pour over the whole fish. Serve immediately.

Chinese FRIED FISH

Serves 10

Once you've collected all the ingredients and premeasured them, this well-flavored dish takes little more than 8 minutes to cook.

1 2-pound black sea bass, cleaned and scaled, head and tail on
2 1-inch slices fresh ginger
1 teaspoon coarse salt
2 tablespoons extra-virgin olive oil
1½ tablespoons chili paste
3 garlic cloves, minced
1 tablespoon Chinese white cooking wine
1 tablespoon Chinese brown vinegar
3 tablespoons Pickled Ginger, chopped (page 125)
1 tablespoon sugar
1 teaspoon cornstarch mixed with ½ cup cold water

Rub the inside and outside of the fish with 1 slice of ginger and the salt.

Heat a wok over high heat and rub the surface with the second slice of ginger. Add 1 tablespoon of the oil and heat. When hot, add the fish to the wok and cook for 1 minute. Turn the fish over and cook 1 minute longer; the fish should be nicely browned. Remove the fish to a platter.

Wash the wok and reheat it over high heat. Add the remaining oil, and when it is hot add the chili paste, garlic, wine, vinegar, pickled ginger, and sugar, stirring well. Replace the fish on top of the sauce, cover the wok, and cook for 2 minutes. Turn the fish over and cook it, covered, for 2 minutes longer. Do not overcook the fish. Remove the fish to a platter. Add the water mixed with the cornstarch to the wok, scraping and stirring the solids together over high heat. Pour the sauce over the fish and serve.

SHRIMP *with* *Ginger and* SCALLION

Serves 10

This entire dish takes less than 3 minutes to cook, and the shrimp taste wonderful.

1 teaspoon Chinese white cooking wine
1 teaspoon sugar
1½ tablespoons soy sauce
⅓ cup extra-virgin olive oil
2 scallions, julienned in 2-inch lengths
3 tablespoons slivered fresh ginger
1 pound medium shrimp in the shell, heads left on

In a small bowl mix the wine, sugar, and soy sauce. Set aside until ready to cook. Heat a wok over high heat, then add the oil. When the oil is hot add the scallions and ginger, and toss for 10 seconds.

Add the shrimp and toss for 2 minutes; the shrimp will turn red. Add the soy sauce mixture and toss for another 10 seconds, then remove from the heat onto a serving plate. Serve immediately.

above: *Lily improvises very well in any kitchen, but if she has a wok and a rice steamer, she can create great dishes. To steam the sea bass, she used my wok and a Japanese grilling rack turned upside down. She then placed the fish in a porcelain baking dish atop the rack, and it steamed perfectly in a matter of minutes.*

left: *All seafood should be absolutely fresh. If you can find shrimp like these with the heads intact, the dish with ginger and scallion will attain its goal of simple, elegant flavor.*

above: *My brother-in-law Stanley Love always had Chinese cooks in his house, and it was at his table that I discovered sweet sausage. I like it cooked with Chinese green beans.* below: *Lightly flavored with chopped ginger and a bit of salt, mustard greens retain their bright flavor.* bottom: *I bought these thin pretty china cups on Canal Street in New York's Chinatown.*

Chopped Tender
MUSTARD GREENS

Serves 10

You can substitute finely cut coriander, flat-leaf parsley, or chervil for the mustard greens.

- 1 pound mustard greens
- 1 tablespoon extra-virgin olive oil
- 1½ teaspoons coarse salt
- 1 teaspoon chopped fresh ginger

Wash and spin-dry the mustard greens. Cut them into ½-inch pieces. Heat a wok over high heat, then add the oil. When the oil is hot add the salt, ginger, and mustard greens. Stir-fry for 2 minutes, remove from the heat onto a serving plate, and serve immediately.

Sweet SAUSAGE
with GREEN BEANS

Serves 10

The sweetness of the Chinese sausage and the slight saltiness of the beans make a very good combination.

- ½ pound Chinese sweet sausage
- 1 pound green beans
- 2½ tablespoons extra-virgin olive oil
- 2 garlic cloves, sliced thick
- 1½ teaspoons coarse salt

Steam the sausage on a rack over simmering water for 15 minutes. Allow it to cool to room temperature, then place it in the refrigerator until cold. The sausage will not slice well if it is not cold. Cut the sausage on the diagonal into ½-inch-thick slices.

Wash the green beans and snap off the stem ends.

Heat a wok over high heat, then add 2 tablespoons of the oil. When the oil is hot add the garlic and salt, stirring for 10 seconds. Then add the green beans and toss constantly for 6 minutes or until the beans are just browned. Immediately remove them from the wok into a serving bowl.

Wash and dry the wok and return it to the burner. Reheat it with the remaining ½ tablespoon of oil. When the oil is hot, add the sausage and stir-fry for 1 minute. Return the green beans to the wok and continue to stir-fry for 1 minute longer. Serve immediately.

Spinach Stems
with BLACK BEANS

Serves 10

Both brown vinegar and water spinach are commonly found in Chinese markets.

- 1½ pounds water spinach, washed, stems intact
- 1 tablespoon extra-virgin olive oil
- 1 teaspoon coarse salt
- 2 garlic cloves, minced
- ½ teaspoon Chinese brown vinegar
- 1 tablespoon fermented black beans
- 1½ tablespoons soy sauce

Wash the water spinach in cold water. Cut off the stems. Save the spinach leaves for another dish. Using the back of a chef's knife, lightly mash the stems. Cut them into 2-inch lengths.

Heat a wok over high heat, then add the oil. When the oil is hot, add the salt and garlic and stir-fry for 30 seconds. Add the vinegar and mix for a few seconds.

Add the black beans and mashed spinach stems, and continue to stir-fry for 1 minute.

Finish by adding the soy sauce and cook, stirring for 30 seconds longer. Remove the mixture from the heat and serve immediately.

Rice with Chinese SAUSAGE *and* Smoked PORK

Serves 10

Here is a very good dish that you can let cook for 30 minutes while you pre-pare some of the ingredients for the rest of the menu's stir-fried recipes.

1 tablespoon extra-virgin olive oil
½ cup diced Chinese sausage
½ cup diced smoked pork
3½ cups uncooked white rice
8 cups water

In a 12-cup heavy stockpot, heat the oil over high heat. Add the Chinese sausage and smoked pork and sauté for 2 minutes until the meat is browned, stirring constantly.

Add the rice and continue sautéing for 1½ minutes.

Add the water and cover with a lid. Bring the water to a boil, then reduce the heat and remove the lid. Allow the rice to cook until almost dry, about 30 minutes. Replace the lid for 1 to 2 minutes longer to steam the rice briefly before serving.

RICE SOUP *with* Coriander LEAVES

Serves 10

I enjoy all the dishes in this menu, but this soup is probably my favorite—it's the epitome of subtlety and simplicity.

15 cups water
1½ cups uncooked white rice
1½ tablespoons coarse salt
¼ cup minced fresh ginger
3 scallions, finely chopped
1¼ cups coriander leaves, washed and chopped
Pickled Ginger (recipe follows)

The rice soup was served with a gar-nish of homemade pickled ginger. I like to keep a big glass jar of this deli-cious condiment in the refrigerator. Very easy to make, it is entirely differ-ent from the pink ginger served in Japanese restaurants: the hot red pepper makes it uniquely Hunanese. Its serving dish was a departure from the celadon color of the rest of the dinnerware, but the ginger looked so beautiful on the red and gold Minton plate that I couldn't resist using it.

In a stockpot combine the water with the rice and bring to a boil. Reduce the heat and simmer, covered, for 1 hour, until the rice has completely softened in an opaque soup. Stir in the salt, ginger, scallions, and 1 cup of the coriander leaves, and then remove from heat.

Serve the soup in individual bowls, using the remaining coriander leaves as garnish. Serve pickled ginger in a separate bowl to accompany the soup.

Pickled Ginger

Serves 10

Many Chinese dishes are accompanied by this tasty ginger; I use it with the Chinese Fried Fish and the Rice Soup.

1 pound fresh ginger, without blemish
1 tablespoon coarse salt
1 tablespoon Chinese grain vinegar
½ cup sugar
½ teaspoon chopped fresh hot red pepper

Peel the ginger with a vegetable peeler, then slice it very thinly. Blanch the gin-ger in boiling water for 20 seconds, then drain. Place it in a bowl and sprin-kle with the salt. Allow it to sit at room temperature for 30 minutes. Drain any liquid that accumulates.

Combine the vinegar and sugar and pour over the ginger. Toss well so that the vinegar coats the ginger. Transfer to a plate and sprinkle with the chopped hot red pepper for garnish.

Made in advance, the ginger can be stored in a covered jar in the refrigerator.

LICHEES *on Ice*

Serves 10

Lichees are amazingly refreshing, especially when served ice cold.

2 bunches fresh lichees (about 40 fruits)
1 serving bowl filled with ice cubes

To prepare the lichees, first remove their stems. Using the point of a sharp knife, cut each fruit to break the hull. Then peel with your fingers.

Arrange the hulled lichees in a mound on top of the ice and serve.

12

"*Fried* Green Tomatoes" B R U N C H

Serves 6

Tennessee *Iced Tea*

Mixed Green Salad

Buttermilk Biscuits with Red Tomatoes

✳ Fried Green *Tomatoes*

Southern *Shrimp* with *Grits*

Nana's Lace *Cookies* ✳ *Ambrosia*

"*Fried* Green Tomatoes"
B R U N C H

I MET SALLI LAGRONE IN NASHVILLE, TENNESSEE, SHORTLY BEFORE MY FIRST BOOK, *ENTERTAINING*, WAS PUBLISHED. SHE WAS AN ACTIVE MEMBER OF THE TOWN'S JUNIOR LEAGUE, WHICH HAD INVITED ME TO SPEAK AT THE HEART OF COUNTRY ANTIQUES SHOW. IT WAS SALLI WHO INTRODUCED ME TO THE ART OF SOUTHERN HOSPITALITY: SHE TOOK ME TO HER HOUSE, COOKED ME GREAT FOOD, AND DROVE ME THROUGH THE COUNTRYSIDE IN SEARCH OF LOCAL BASKETRY, BAR-BECUE, HUSH PUPPIES, AND MAGNOLIAS. IN SUBSEQUENT YEARS SALLI HAS COME NORTH TO VISIT, AND I HAVE CONTINUED MY FORAYS INTO THE SOUTH, TRADING RECIPES, GARDEN KNOWLEDGE, AND OUT-OF-THE-WAY SECRET SOURCES. WE HAVE BECOME KINDRED SPIRITS. ON A RECENT WEEKEND IN CONNECTICUT, SALLI AND I COOKED THIS BRUNCH MENU. IT REFLECTS HER ABILITY TO TAKE OLD-FASHIONED RECIPES AND MAKE THEM BRIGHTER AND BETTER THAN THE ORIGINALS. EVIDENCE THE SHRIMP ON GRITS: THIS DISH IS OFTEN BROWNISH AND NOT SO ATTRACTIVE, BUT SALLI ADDS CHOPPED FLAT-LEAF PARSLEY FOR COLOR AND FRESH THYME FOR TASTE. SHE FRIES HER GREEN TOMATOES IN CANOLA OIL INSTEAD OF LARD, AND AS A RESULT THEY ARE LIGHTER AND MORE TENDER. AND HER AMBROSIA IS JUST THAT—THE FRESHEST ASSEMBLAGE OF CITRUS AND COCONUT!

previous page: *There were lots of green tomatoes in the garden when Salli came to Westport. She helped me make green tomato mincemeat and piccalilli, and my mother took many sparklingly fresh tomatoes home to pickle in brine.*

above: *Shrimp on grits is a common brunch favorite in the South, where along the coast the crustaceans are found in abundance. Salli prefers fresh medium shrimp and insists that they be sautéed in bacon fat for flavor.*

"There is no compromise in a menu of this sort," Salli says. "Flavors must be authentic!"

Tennessee
ICED TEA
*Makes 8 to 10
8 - ounce servings*

A fresh-tasting punch like this one is even better if a wonderful tea is used. I prefer a rose Pouchong or any of the fruit-flavored blends from Fortnum & Mason.

Chipped ice
1 quart fresh orange juice
1 quart fresh-brewed tea, cooled
2 tablespoons honey
¾ cup golden rum, such as Mount Gay
1 orange, sliced thinly crosswise and quartered

Fill a large pitcher with chipped ice and stir in the orange juice, tea, honey, and rum (you may need to use two pitchers). Serve over ice in tall glasses and garnish with orange slices.

Mixed
GREEN SALAD
Serves 6

When toasting the pecans, shake the baking sheet once or twice to ensure even toasting.

1 cup whole shelled pecans
6 tablespoons extra-virgin olive oil
3 tablespoons champagne vinegar with tarragon
Salt and freshly ground pepper
2 heads radicchio, leaves separated, washed, and dried well
1 head chicory, leaves separated, washed, and dried well
2 heads Belgian endive, leaves separated, washed, and dried well

Preheat the oven to 300° F.

On a baking sheet lined with parchment paper, spread the pecans evenly and toast for 8 minutes or just until they become fragrant; watch that they don't burn.

In a small bowl, whisk together the olive oil, vinegar, and salt and pepper to taste.

Tear the radicchio and chicory into manageable pieces; keep the endive leaves whole. Toss the greens with the dressing and arrange on six individual plates. Sprinkle each salad with toasted pecans.

Buttermilk
BISCUITS *with* RED TOMATOES
Makes 2 dozen biscuits

I've always been told that the secret to flaky biscuits is a light touch.

3 cups unbleached all-purpose flour
4 teaspoons baking powder
½ teaspoon baking soda
1 teaspoon salt
10 tablespoons unsalted butter, chilled and cut in pieces
1 cup plus 2 tablespoons buttermilk
½ cup (1 stick) unsalted butter, melted
2 large tomatoes, sliced and quartered
Salt and freshly ground pepper

Preheat the oven to 425° F. Line a baking sheet with parchment paper.

In a large mixing bowl, sift together the flour, baking powder, baking soda, and salt.

Using a pastry cutter, two knives, or your fingertips, blend in the chilled butter until the mixture resembles coarse meal. Stir in the buttermilk and mix just until the dough holds together. Turn the dough out on a lightly floured surface and knead briefly until it is smooth. Roll out the dough ½ inch thick and cut into rounds using a 2-inch biscuit cutter.

Place the biscuits on the baking sheet. Prick the tops with a fork and brush with the melted butter. Bake for 12 to 15 minutes, just until lightly golden. Transfer the biscuits to a wire rack to cool. Cut the biscuits crosswise in half and fill with a slice of tomato sprinkled with coarse salt and pepper.

Fried Green
TOMATOES
Serves 6

Try to find large, uniformly sized tomatoes and cut them in even slices.

3 tablespoons unbleached all-purpose flour
½ cup yellow cornmeal
1 teaspoon coarse salt
1 teaspoon freshly ground pepper
½ cup canola oil
4 large green tomatoes, cut into ½-inch-thick slices

In a shallow bowl, mix together the flour, cornmeal, salt, and pepper.

In a large sauté pan heat the canola oil over medium heat until hot, but not smoking. Dredge the tomato slices in the cornmeal mixture. Fry in the oil until golden brown, 3 to 5 minutes per side. Remove the tomato slices with a slotted spatula and drain on paper towels briefly. Serve hot.

left: *Salli's fried green tomatoes are every bit as tempting as those in Fannie Flagg's novel,* Fried Green Tomatoes at the Whistle Stop Café. *Lightly coated with cornmeal and gently fried until golden, these were delicious!*

above: *My daughter, Alexis, found these Depression glasses called "Fiestamates" on Long Island. The brightly painted rims brighten any drink.*
left: *The mixed green salad was served on a Fiestaware salad plate. I used my precious green Bakelite flatware for brunch; it is a rather uncommon color for these collectibles.*

right: *Salli picked small, very red tomatoes from my garden and sliced them to just the right thickness for the buttermilk biscuits.*

Southern SHRIMP *with* GRITS

Serves 6

The rich flavor of this shrimp balances wonderfully with the blandness of the grits.

12 slices smoked, lean bacon
    Unsalted butter (if needed)
 2 large onions, quartered and thinly sliced
 1 medium green or red pepper, seeded and cut in strips
 2 garlic cloves, minced
 1 jalapeño pepper, seeded and minced
½ cup unbleached all-purpose flour
 3 pounds (about 60) medium shrimp, peeled and deveined
 3 cups water
 2 tablespoons Worcestershire sauce
 2 teaspoons soy sauce
    Juice of ½ lemon
    Tabasco sauce
 1 tablespoon chopped thyme leaves
 2 tablespoons chopped parsley
    Salt and freshly ground pepper
    White Grits (recipe follows)

In a heavy skillet cook the bacon over medium heat until brown. With tongs, transfer the bacon to paper towels to drain, reserving the bacon fat in the pan. There should be about 5 tablespoons of fat; if there is less, add enough butter to reach that amount. When the bacon has cooled, crumble it and set aside.

Add the onions, pepper, garlic, and jalapeño pepper to the skillet and cook over medium heat until soft, about 3 to 5 minutes. Remove them to a bowl with a slotted spoon and set aside, reserving the fat again.

Pour the flour onto a plate and dredge the shrimp lightly in the flour. Reheat the bacon fat and brown the shrimp over medium heat for 2 to 3 minutes. Remove them from the pan with a slotted spoon and set aside on a plate.

Return the onions, pepper, and garlic to the pan. Sprinkle with 2 tablespoons of the flour and sauté over medium heat to brown. Add the water, Worcestershire sauce, soy sauce, lemon juice, and Tabasco sauce. Simmer uncovered for 30 minutes over low heat.

Add the shrimp, thyme, and 1 tablespoon of the parsley to the skillet. Season with salt and pepper and continue cooking over low heat for 20 minutes, adding water as needed to create a thick sauce.

Serve the mixture over hot white grits and sprinkle with the crumbled bacon and remaining parsley.

White Grits

Serves 6

 6 cups water
1½ cups white grits
 1 teaspoon coarse salt

In a large, heavy saucepan bring the water to a boil over medium-high heat and stir in the grits and salt. Cover the pot and reduce the heat to a simmer. Allow the grits to simmer until all the liquid is absorbed, stirring occasionally, about 30 minutes.

Nana's Lace COOKIES

Makes 3 dozen cookies

Salli's grandmother gave her the recipe for these crispy treats.

½ cup unbleached all-purpose flour
¼ teaspoon baking powder
½ cup sugar
½ cup old-fashioned rolled oats
 1 tablespoon orange zest
½ cup toasted pecans, chopped (page 130)
 2 tablespoons heavy cream
 6 tablespoons (¾ stick) unsalted butter, melted
 2 tablespoons light corn syrup

Preheat the oven to 325° F.

Line one or more baking sheets with parchment paper.

In a large mixing bowl, mix together the flour, baking powder, sugar, rolled oats, orange zest, and pecans. Stir in the cream, melted butter, and corn syrup until well blended.

Using a teaspoon, drop spoonfuls of the batter 2 inches apart onto the baking sheet and bake until light brown, about 8 minutes. Remove the baking sheet from the oven and allow the cookies to stand only until just cool enough to handle. They must still be hot when they are transferred from the sheet. Remove the cookies with a spatula and quickly drape them over a lightly buttered rolling pin to cool. When they have cooled completely, slide the cookies off the rolling pin. Store them in a tin container.

AMBROSIA

Serves 6

*Serving just the flesh of these fruits
makes this ambrosia especially delicate.*

3 pink grapefruits
3 white grapefruits
6 seedless oranges
  Meat of ½ fresh coconut,
  removed from shell and peeled

Using a very sharp stainless-steel paring knife, slice off the stem and tip of one grapefruit. Working from top to bottom, cut away the peel in long strokes. With the peeled grapefruit in hand, and working over a bowl, slide the knife down the sides of each segment, cutting the flesh away from the white membrane. Twist the blade under the segment to lift it out, and place it in the bowl. Continue until all segments are removed. Squeeze the juice from the remaining membrane over the fruit to keep it moist. Repeat with the remaining grapefruits and the oranges. Arrange the segments on a platter. Using a vegetable peeler, shave the coconut into long strips. Mound the coconut in the center of the platter.

opposite: *Salli and I walked through the early-autumn garden and picked as we walked: crabapples, nasturtiums, colorful French pumpkins (potirons), and chartreuse green quince. From these findings she and I concocted colorful arrangements for the table and sideboard.* **above:** *Salli's ambrosia is made with grapefruits, oranges, and freshly shredded coconut.* **right:** *Nana's Lace Cookies must be cooled, curved, on a lightly buttered rolling pin.*

13

Midsummer *fiesta*

Serves 10 to 12

Grapefruit Margaritas

✻ Mexican *Fish* Soup

Salsa *Cruda* ✻ Grilled *Quesadillas*

Tamales with *Chili-Corn Filling*

Red Cabbage and *Mango* Salad

Almond Sponge Cake with Wine-Poached *Plums*

Midsummer *fiesta*

EVERYONE LOVES MEXICAN FOOD. EVEN THOSE FOLKS WHO COMPLAIN THAT IT'S TOO SPICY WILL BE OBSERVED EATING GREAT BIG MOUNDS OF NACHOS OR WEDGE AFTER WEDGE OF QUESADILLAS AT A PARTY. THERE ARE MANY EXTRAORDINARILY TASTY AND EASY MEXICAN DISHES THAT EVEN THE FUSSIEST GUEST WILL DEVOUR. BUT IT IS ESSENTIAL THAT ALL THE INGREDIENTS BE IMPECCABLY FRESH AND THE FRUITS AND VEGETABLES PERFECTLY RIPE. UNFORTUNATELY, MUCH OF THE MEXICAN FOOD IN RESTAURANTS NORTH OF THE BORDER IS OF THE FAST FOOD VARIETY—CANNED BEANS, PREPARED SALSAS, AND MASS-PRODUCED TORTILLAS AND CHIPS. AT MY WEEKEND HOUSE IN EAST HAMPTON, WHERE I OFTEN SERVE THIS SIMPLE MENU, I SHOP AHEAD FOR THE AVOCADOS AND MANGOES SO THAT THEY WILL BE AT THE PEAK OF RIPENESS FOR THE SOUP, GUACAMOLE, AND SALADS. THE QUESADILLAS CAN BE ASSEMBLED AN HOUR OR TWO IN ADVANCE OF THE GUESTS' ARRIVAL AND COOKED ON THE SPOT TO ORDER. THE SOUP IS BEST MADE AT THE LAST MINUTE, BUT ALL THE INGREDIENTS CAN BE CHOPPED AND KEPT CHILLED IN THE REFRIGERATOR UNTIL READY TO COOK. I LIKE TO BAKE THE ALMOND CAKE EARLY ON THE DAY OF THE PARTY. APRICOTS, PLUMS, OR PEACHES, SLICED AND SIMMERED IN A SWEET DESSERT WINE, ARE A DELICIOUS TOPPING FOR THE CAKE.

previous page: *I buy my sunflowers from Mr. Babinski, a local farmer in Bridgehampton who grows all sizes. I put masses of them in big jars on all the tables on my porch.* above: *Perhaps my favorite part of this meal is the grapefruit margarita. I was introduced to unusual margaritas at Rosa Mexicana, a superb Mexican restaurant in New York City. There the drink of choice is a pink pomegranate tequila drink that is served frozen; this citrus version rivals the pink.*

Midsummer *fiesta*

Grapefruit MARGARITAS

Serves 10 to 12

Be sure the grapefruits are fresh and the tequila is of the highest quality. The recipe is made in three batches.

Chipped ice
4 cups fresh grapefruit juice
3 limes, juiced
2 cups tequila
¾ cup Grand Marnier
1 cup sugar
Coarse salt
1 lime, sliced, for garnish
Mint sprigs, for garnish

Fill a blender jar with chipped ice.
Add one third of the grapefruit juice, lime juice, tequila, Grand Marnier, and sugar. Blend at top speed until frothy. Pour into 3 or 4 chilled or salt-rimmed glasses and garnish with a lime slice and a sprig of mint. Repeat twice with the remaining ingredients.

Mexican FISH SOUP

Serves 10

The spiciness of this broth is tempered by the large pieces of avocado and wedges of lime.

2 tablespoons extra-virgin olive oil
2 medium onions, chopped
4 garlic cloves, chopped
1 pound fresh Italian tomatoes, seeded and crushed
4 carrots, peeled and diced
4 celery stalks, diced
1 green bell pepper, seeded and chopped
10 cups water
Salt and freshly ground pepper
2 medium potatoes, peeled and diced

1 3-pound snapper, filleted and cut in chunks
20 medium shrimp, cleaned and deveined
1 pound cleaned squid, sliced into 1-inch pieces
24 oysters, shucked
Salsa Cruda (recipe follows)
2 avocados, peeled and sliced
2 limes, cut into eighths
Tabasco sauce

Heat the oil in a large skillet over medium heat. Add the onions and garlic, and sauté until translucent, 5 to 7 minutes.
Add the tomatoes, carrots, celery, green pepper, water, and salt and pepper. Bring to a boil, then reduce the heat to medium-low and cook for 15 minutes, uncovered.
Add the potatoes and cook for 20 minutes or until tender.
Add the snapper and simmer about 2 minutes. The soup can be prepared to this point up to 5 hours in advance and kept covered in the refrigerator.
When ready to serve, bring the soup to a boil and add the shrimp, squid, and oysters. Return to the boil, then remove from the heat immediately and let stand for 1 minute to finish cooking the seafood.
Spoon into shallow soup bowls and add a spoonful of Salsa Cruda to each serving. Garnish each serving with a few slices of avocado.
Serve with lime wedges and Tabasco sauce.

SALSA *Cruda*

Makes 2 cups

3 very ripe tomatoes, seeded and diced
1 jalapeño pepper, seeded and minced
1 large white onion, diced
Salt and freshly ground pepper

In a mixing bowl, combine the tomatoes, jalapeño, onion, and salt and pepper. Mix well.

Grilled QUESADILLAS

Serves 10

Once they're browned and the filling is melted, the easiest way to cut quesadillas is with kitchen scissors.

1 red bell pepper
1 yellow bell pepper
1 green bell pepper
2 Italian hot peppers, seeded and sliced
5 tablespoons extra-virgin olive oil
2 red onions, thinly sliced
½ pound sharp yellow cheddar cheese, grated
½ pound Monterey Jack cheese, grated
10 large (10-inch) flour tortillas
2 tomatoes, thinly sliced
1 can sardines, drained
1 cup cilantro leaves, chopped
Salt and freshly ground pepper
Guacamole (recipe follows)

Roast the bell and hot peppers over a gas flame or in the broiler (page 150). Peel, seed, and slice thinly.
Heat 2 tablespoons of the oil in a large skillet over medium-low heat. Add the red onions and sauté until just tender, 3 to 4 minutes.

138

left: *One of my friends, Marie Mendez, taught me to make quesadillas from her mother's recipe: whole sardines, roasted peppers, Monterey Jack cheese, and yellow cheddar. Fresh cilantro leaves are very important. Another delicious filling consists of sliced ripe tomatoes, mozzarella cheese, and cilantro.*

above: *For a large group I heat several pans on my stove top and cook three or more quesadillas at a time. This keeps guests satisfied and no one has to wait very long for these delicious appetizers. This tortilla is filled with sautéed sweet red onion, two kinds of cheese, sardines, and cilantro leaves.*

above: *My daughter, Alexis, has amassed a huge collection of Fire King china and she gave me twenty-four of everything for parties. The Mexican fish soup was served in large flat bowls.*
right: *Round English breadboards make excellent serving "plates" for the ten-inch quesadillas.*

In a mixing bowl combine the cheddar cheese and the Monterey Jack cheese.

Heat 1 or more skillets over medium-high heat. Add ½ teaspoon of the oil to each pan to coat. Place a tortilla in each skillet and sprinkle liberally with the grated cheeses. Arrange some of the peppers, onions, tomatoes, or sardines, in any combination you choose, on top of the cheese. Sprinkle with cilantro, salt, and pepper, then top with a second tortilla. Cook for 2 minutes, then flip the quesadilla (see Note) and cook the other side for 2 more minutes. Slide the quesadilla onto a plate or rack. Repeat with the remaining ingredients.

Using a pair of kitchen scissors, cut the quesadillas into eighths and serve with guacamole and additional chopped cilantro.

Note: It may be easier to turn the quesadilla by inverting it onto a plate, then sliding it back into the skillet.

Guacamole

Makes 1½ cups

Juice of 1 lime
4 garlic cloves, minced
5 scallions, white part only, chopped
1 cup cilantro, finely chopped
1 jalapeño pepper, seeded and minced
3 ripe avocados, pitted and peeled

In a mixing bowl, combine the lime juice, garlic, scallions, cilantro, and jalapeño. Using a fork, lightly mash the avocados into the mixture, leaving some large chunks.

Serve with chips or as a garnish for the quesadillas.

TAMALES *with* CHILI-CORN FILLING

Makes 12

Tamales can be prepared in advance and frozen. When ready to serve, just warm them, wrapped in foil, in the oven.

12 ears corn
2 cups fine ground cornmeal
2 teaspoons double-acting baking powder
1 teaspoon coarse salt
⅓ cup lard, softened
1½ cups chicken stock, preferably homemade
Chili-Corn Filling
(recipe follows)

Husk the corn, reserving the husks. Soak the husks in hot water for 5 minutes, drain, and set aside.

Scrape the kernels of corn into a large bowl. Set aside 2 cups of kernels and reserve the rest for another use.

In a bowl, combine the cornmeal, baking powder, and salt.

Using an electric mixer, whip the lard until it is fluffy, starting on low speed and gradually increasing the speed to high. Add the cornmeal mixture 2 tablespoons at a time until well combined.

While the mixer is still running, gradually add the stock until well combined. Stop the mixer and test a small amount of dough to see if it floats in a

above: *Tamales are not difficult to make, but the dough must be beaten to an ethereal lightness before it is seasoned and wrapped in the corn husk. I served the tamales on a shallow plate lined with fresh corn husks.*

glass of water. If it does not, continue beating until the dough floats. Gently fold in 1 cup of the corn kernels.

Pick through the corn husks and find twelve 4 by 9-inch pieces. Lay them out flat and spread 2 tablespoons of the dough on the interior of each husk in a 3 by 4-inch rectangle.

Put 1 tablespoon of the Chili-Corn Filling in the center of each dough-lined husk. Fold the sides of the corn husk to the center, then fold over the ends, overlapping them. Use kitchen string to tie the top end closed.

Layer the tamales, seam side down, in a steamer rack or a flat-bottomed colander. Fill the bottom half of the steamer with water up to within 1 inch of the base of the rack or colander. Bring the water to a boil and cover tightly. Reduce the heat and simmer for 1 to 1½ hours, until the dough is firm enough to pull away easily from the corn husks. Serve the tamales in the husks on a heated platter.

Chili-Corn Filling

Makes enough for 12 tamales

2 poblano chilis, roasted (page 150)
1 large onion, minced
2 garlic cloves, minced
¼ cup vegetable oil
1 cup corn kernels
2 tablespoons chopped cilantro leaves
Salt and freshly ground pepper

Seed and chop the roasted poblano chilis, and set aside.

In a large heavy skillet, cook the onion and the garlic in the oil over moderate heat, stirring, until they are softened and golden. Add the corn kernels and cook the mixture, stirring occasionally, for 5 minutes. Add the chilis and salt and pepper to taste, and heat through.

Red CABBAGE and MANGO SALAD

Serves 10

A semi-sweet vinegar dressing is appropriate for this salad. I prefer the taste of Japanese rice vinegar for salads that include fruit. It is light, very tasty, and unusual.

2 ripe mangoes
2 small heads red cabbage, shredded
3 large tomatoes, sliced

Dressing

¼ cup Japanese rice vinegar (plain, not seasoned)
⅓ cup light olive oil
3 tablespoons sesame oil
½ teaspoon sugar
2 tablespoons finely chopped cilantro leaves
Salt and freshly ground pepper

To easily dice the mangoes, cut down both flat sides of the fruit, avoiding the mango pit inside. Using a sharp knife, slice the flesh of the mango halves on the diagonal in one direction and then in the opposite direction without cutting through the skin. With your fingers, gently force the mango inside out, allowing the cubes to separate. Reserve 1 mango half; cut the cubes from the remaining 3 halves.

In a medium bowl, whisk together the rice vinegar, olive oil, sesame oil, sugar, cilantro, and salt and pepper.

In a large bowl, toss the cabbage and mango cubes with the dressing. Arrange the tomato slices in a circle in the center of the salad. Garnish with the reserved cubed mango half. Serve immediately.

left: *I love mixing tropical fruits with salad. Here sweet ripe mangoes are mixed with red cabbage. I added sliced tomatoes and tossed it all with a rice wine vinaigrette.* **right:** *I set small tables on my front porch. Since the trim of my East Hampton house is teal blue-green, I bought used wooden chairs from a rental center, painted them a bright teal, and covered the seats with chartreuse vinyl.*

left: *Two years ago I discovered a type of plum called the dinosaur egg. It is mauve-purple with red streaks on the skins and a very deep red flesh inside. Juicy and sweet, it is great for eating as well as cooking.*
opposite: *After baking and cooling, the almond cake sank in the middle, creating a perfect indentation for the plum slices. Use whatever shape tube pan you fancy—round, rectangular, or square. The confectioners' sugar and sweet wine syrup are the finishing touches to this delicious cake.*

Almond SPONGE CAKE *with Wine-Poached* PLUMS

Serves 10

I used an unusual square tube pan for this almond cake.

1 cup blanched almonds, ground fine
1 cup sugar
¼ teaspoon baking powder
1 tablespoon unbleached all-purpose flour
5 large eggs, separated
1 pinch salt
  Confectioners' sugar for dusting
2 dinosaur egg plums, or 4 small Italian plums (see Note)
¼ cup sweet dessert wine, such as Sauternes or Marsala

Preheat the oven to 325° F.

Line the bottom of a 10-inch tube pan with parchment paper. Butter and flour it, tapping out the excess flour.

In a large mixing bowl, combine the almonds, sugar, baking powder, and flour, mixing well.

In the bowl of an electric mixer, beat the egg whites with the salt until stiff but not dry. Add one egg yolk at a time and continue beating until they are all incorporated. Beating at low speed, add the almond–sugar mixture gradually, mixing just until all the ingredients are blended.

Pour the batter into the prepared pan and bake for 35 to 40 minutes, or until a cake tester inserted in the middle comes out clean. Cool the cake in the pan on a rack.

Remove the cake from the pan without inverting it. The top will settle. Lightly dust the cake with confectioners' sugar.

Slice the plums thin. In a sauté pan, heat the dessert wine over medium heat until hot. Add the plum slices and cook for 2 to 3 minutes, until just tender and warm.

Remove the fruit with a slotted spoon and arrange the plums on top of the cake. Continue cooking the wine over medium heat until it is reduced by one-fourth and is syrupy, about 10 minutes. Pour over the plums and serve.

Note: Dinosaur egg plums are quite a bit larger than Italian plums, so adjust the quantity accordingly if you are using the smaller variety.

14

PASTA *for a* Crowd

Serves 20

Grilled, Roasted, and Marinated *Antipasto*

✳ *Focaccia* with a Variety of Toppings

Assorted *Pastas* Made to Order

Italian Cornmeal Cake ✳ Poached Blood *Oranges*

Ricotta Ice Cream

PASTA *for a Crowd*

MANY YEARS AGO I WAS INVITED TO A FRIEND'S FOR DINNER. I WAS TOLD THE PASTA WOULD BE SPECTACULAR AND THAT ELI ZABAR WAS COOKING. ELI HAD JUST OPENED HIS SHOP, E.A.T., ON MADISON AVENUE, AND IT WAS ALREADY KNOWN AS ONE OF NEW YORK'S BEST FOOD STORES. WE WERE SERVED ABOUT SEVEN DIFFERENT PASTAS, EACH UNIQUE AND DELICIOUS. AS SOON AS EACH DISH WAS COMPLETED IT WAS OFFERED TO THE GUESTS FROM A HUGE PLATTER. FOR YEARS I TRIED TO THINK OF A WAY TO PRESENT SUCH PASTAS TO A LARGER GROUP WITHOUT RUNNING THE RISK OF ANNOYING GUESTS WITH INORDINATE DELAYS. THIS BUFFET ALLOWS ME TO SERVE VARIED HOT PASTA TO A CROWD. IT IS AN INVENT-YOUR-OWN DINNER, A PARTY WITH A BIT OF DRAMA ATTACHED AS GUESTS SELECT THEIR FLAVORS AND WATCH THEIR INVENTIONS TAKE FORM RIGHT AT THE STOVE. IT IS IMPORTANT TO CONSIDER WHERE THIS DINNER WILL BE PREPARED. IT IS BEST IF YOU HAVE A KITCHEN WITH AN ISLAND WHERE GUESTS CAN GATHER, CHOOSE, AND WATCH. A COUNTER-TYPE KITCHEN WITH A SEPARATE STOVE CAN ALSO WORK WELL, BUT IT IS NOT AS THEATRICAL. FOR A LARGE PARTY, PORTABLE STOVES OR BURNERS CAN BE SET UP ON SERVING TABLES ON WHICH THE INGREDIENTS ARE ARRANGED. I'VE ALSO DONE THIS TYPE OF PARTY WITH OMELETS AND BLINIS.

left: *In my kitchen I have a four-burner counter range set in a marble and galvanized-steel island; my many copper pots and pans are suspended from above.* right and below: *Standing behind the stove with tongs, I could reach any of the yellowware bowls filled with the myriad ingredients for cooked-to-order pastas.*

I discovered that guests really like experimenting with pasta toppings. They are not afraid to try various mushrooms—for example, cremini or porcini—fresh bitter greens such as swiss chard and escarole, butternut squash, or pine nuts and cilantro.

right: *I found wonderful ravioli at New York's Dean and DeLuca. Some were round, some square, but all were tender pieces of pasta filled with delicate and beautifully seasoned mixtures. I especially liked the tomato ravioli filled with ricotta.*

previous page: *At one end of my kitchen island I set out a large antipasto array, and on the rest of the counter were the precooked pastas, the cut-up vegetables, and the other prepared items that were used to make the flavorful pasta entrées.*

left: *One guest asked for egg and tomato ravioli topped with porcini mushrooms and swiss chard. I sautéed the vegetables in olive oil, seasoned them with a bit of fresh rosemary, added the precooked ravioli, and served a perfect, fresh pasta dish in a matter of a very few minutes.*

Grilled, Roasted, and Marinated ANTIPASTO

Serves 20

The antipasto was made so it would not compete with the pasta toppings; I tried hard not to repeat ingredients. I also included grilled, marinated, and roasted dishes to offer more variety. The antipasto will keep at least twenty guests happy and occupied, but you can adjust the amounts to take into account your guest list and your recipe preferences.

Marinated Chick-peas

- 1 pound dried chick-peas, picked over
- 4 garlic cloves, crushed
- 3 bay leaves
- 1 sprig rosemary
- 1 sprig thyme

Marinade

- Juice of 2 lemons
- ¼ cup thyme leaves, chopped
- 3 garlic cloves, slivered
- Salt and freshly ground pepper

Soak the chick-peas in enough cold water to cover for 12 hours, changing the water every 5 to 8 hours. Drain the chick-peas.

In a saucepan, add the chick-peas, fresh water to cover, garlic, bay leaves, rosemary, and thyme. Simmer over medium-low heat for 1½ hours, or until tender. Drain the chick-peas, discard the seasonings, and set aside in a large bowl to cool. To make the marinade, in a small bowl, whisk together the lemon juice, thyme, and garlic. Add salt and pepper to taste. Pour the mixture over the chick-peas and toss thoroughly. Allow them to marinate for a few hours covered in the refrigerator before serving.

Roasted Shallots

- 1 tablespoon extra-virgin olive oil
- 1 tablespoon balsamic vinegar
- 1 tablespoon dark brown sugar
- 2 pounds shallots, peeled, point ends intact

Preheat the oven to 500° F.

In a large bowl, whisk together the olive oil, vinegar, and brown sugar. Toss the peeled shallots in the marinade and spread evenly in a roasting pan. Roast for 20 to 25 minutes, tossing every 5 minutes. Serve hot or at room temperature.

Grilled Zucchini

- 3 medium zucchini
- ¼ cup rice vinegar
- Fresh dill sprigs, chopped

Cut the zucchini in half crosswise, then cut each piece in half lengthwise. Over medium-high heat grill the zucchini on a cast-iron grill pan for 3 minutes per side. Transfer the zucchini to a serving dish and sprinkle with the rice vinegar. Garnish with chopped fresh dill sprigs.

Grilled Eggplant

- 8 small Italian eggplants, cut lengthwise in ½-inch slices
- ¼ cup coarse salt
- 2 tablespoons balsamic vinegar
- 1 tablespoon extra-virgin olive oil
- 1 teaspoon marjoram leaves, chopped
- 1 tablespoon rosemary leaves, chopped
- Salt and freshly ground pepper

Rub the cut surfaces of the eggplant with salt (see Note). Keep in a glass or steel dish, cut side up, for 30 minutes. The salt helps remove any bitterness.

Rinse the eggplant, drain, and pat dry with paper towels.

In a cast-iron grill pan over medium-high heat, grill the eggplant for 2 minutes per side until just tender and lightly browned.

Toss the eggplant in a large bowl with the balsamic vinegar, olive oil, marjoram, rosemary, salt, and pepper, and serve hot or at room temperature.

Note: If using very tender Violetta eggplants, the salting is unnecessary. Slice eggplants lengthwise on an electric slicer ½ inch thick for quick results.

Marinated Black Olives

- 2 cups large black olives
- Zest of 1 lemon
- 2 teaspoons chopped fresh thyme leaves
- 1 teaspoon coarsely ground pepper
- 2 tablespoons extra-virgin olive oil

In a mixing bowl, toss together the black olives, lemon zest, thyme, pepper, and olive oil. Transfer to a bowl and serve.

opposite: *Homemade marinated olives, grilled zucchini and eggplant slices, and roasted peppers were some of the antipasto ingredients, while cheeses, vegetables, herbs, and olive oil were used for the pasta toppings.*

Roasted Pearl Onions

½ pound red pearl onions, peeled
½ pound white pearl onions, peeled
½ pound yellow pearl onions, peeled
2 tablespoons extra-virgin olive oil
Salt and freshly ground pepper

Marinade

2 tablespoons extra-virgin olive oil
2 teaspoons balsamic vinegar
1 teaspoon rosemary leaves, finely chopped
1 teaspoon thyme leaves, finely chopped

Preheat the oven to 500° F.

In a large bowl, toss the onions in the olive oil; sprinkle with salt and pepper. Spread the onions in a large stainless-steel roasting pan. Roast for 20 minutes until golden brown. In a small bowl, whisk together the olive oil, vinegar, rosemary, and thyme. Toss the hot roasted onions in the marinade and allow to marinate for 30 minutes or longer before serving. Serve at room temperature.

Marinated Green Olives

2 cups large green olives
Zest of 1 orange
2 garlic cloves, slivered
1 tablespoon chopped fresh rosemary
2 teaspoons extra-virgin olive oil
Freshly ground pepper

In a mixing bowl, toss together the olives, orange zest, garlic, rosemary, olive oil, and pepper to taste. Transfer to a serving bowl.

Grilled Fennel

Fennel is a licorice-flavored vegetable that has a ferny top and a thick white bulbous base. It is the white base that is used for grilling and sautéing.

2 large fennel bulbs, trimmed of tops and sliced thin, top to bottom
1 tablespoon chopped fresh chervil
1 tablespoon extra-virgin olive oil
Salt and freshly ground pepper

Using a cast-iron grill pan, grill the fennel slices over medium-high heat for 3 to 5 minutes per side, until just tender and browned. Toss them in a large bowl with the chervil, olive oil, and salt and pepper to taste. Transfer to a serving platter.

Roasted Red Peppers

After roasting the peppers, I prefer to rub or peel their skins off. Some people wash the skins off, but I find that water takes away some of the flavor.

4 red bell peppers
1 tablespoon balsamic vinegar
Salt and freshly ground pepper

To roast the peppers, skewer them on a long fork and hold them over a gas flame, or place them in a broiler. Turn them to char until the entire skin is uniformly black. Remove from the flame or broiler and wrap each pepper in a piece of paper toweling.

After the peppers have "sweated" for 5 to 10 minutes, rub off the blackened skin, remove the seeds and stems, and cut into quarters.

Toss the peppers in a mixing bowl with the balsamic vinegar, salt, and pepper and serve.

FOCACCIA

Makes 12 servings

This crunchy bread is subtly flavored with rosemary. It is made in individual rounds that can be topped with a number of delicious ingredients.

2 cups water
1½ tablespoons rosemary leaves
1⅓ tablespoons active dry yeast
6 cups unbleached all-purpose flour
⅔ cup extra-virgin olive oil, plus extra for oiling and brushing
1 tablespoon coarse salt
3 tablespoons chopped fresh thyme leaves
3 tablespoons chopped fresh rosemary leaves
Focaccia Topping of choice (suggestions follow)

In a saucepan bring 1⅓ cups of the water to a boil over medium-high heat and pour over the whole rosemary leaves in a large mixing bowl. Allow to steep for 30 minutes. Strain out the rosemary and pour the lukewarm water into the bowl of an electric mixer. Add the yeast and let stand for 10 minutes, until foamy.

Gradually stir in 4 cups of the flour, forming a soft dough. Knead with a dough hook or by hand for 10 minutes. Form the dough into a ball. Oil a large mixing bowl and place the dough in it, rotating the dough to cover it with oil. Cover the bowl with plastic wrap and allow the dough to rise until doubled in bulk, about 2 to 3 hours.

Punch down the dough and add in the remaining flour, water, ⅔ cup of the olive oil, salt, thyme, and chopped rosemary. Turn out on a lightly floured surface and knead until the dough is smooth and elastic. Return the dough to an oiled bowl, cover with plastic wrap, and allow to rise a second time until doubled, about 2 to 3 hours.

Preheat the oven to 400° F., and line baking sheets with parchment paper.

Divide the dough into 12 pieces. Flatten each into a round and arrange on the baking sheets. Brush each focaccia with olive oil and press toppings into the center. Bake for 20 minutes until golden brown.

Focaccia Toppings

Top your focaccia with one of the following suggestions, or create your own combination, always using fresh ingredients. Experiment to taste with the amounts of each ingredient used.

* Roasted red peppers, cut into thin strips, with marjoram, coarse salt, pepper, and olive oil

* Sun-dried tomatoes, with fresh chopped rosemary, coarse salt, pepper, and olive oil

* Black olives, sautéed fennel, and caramelized red onions
  (To caramelize the onions, sauté 3 red onions in 3 tablespoons unsalted butter, 1 tablespoon sugar, and a pinch of coarse salt for 10 minutes over medium heat. Add 1 tablespoon very good balsamic vinegar and cook an additional 6 minutes.)

* Roasted red peppers, sun-dried tomatoes, and roasted Italian green peppers, with coarse salt, pepper, and olive oil

* Paper-thin slices of yellow onion and tomato, with oregano leaves and slivers of garlic

The focaccia for this dinner are small and puffy. Served as individual portions, the tasty bread is flavored with toppings of roasted red peppers, onions, fennel, and rosemary. Coarse salt and freshly ground black pepper give an added pungency to this favorite bread.

Assorted PASTAS Made to Order

Here are some pastas that look good and taste wonderful. Have as many as possible on hand, precooked, drained, and tossed with olive oil, so your guests have a variety from which to choose. Allow a total of one-quarter to one-half pound of pasta per person. This permits each guest to choose three or four different dishes as a sampling, which is the whole reason for this meal.

* Tomato ravioli filled with ricotta
* Spinach ravioli filled with beets
* Egg ravioli filled with veal and thyme
* Round egg ravioli filled with cheese
* Tagliardi *(thick squares of egg pasta)*
* Bretelloni *(wide ruffled noodles that hold sauce well)*
* Orrechiette *(egg, tomato, beet, or spinach ear-shaped pasta)*
* Gidi del Gargano *(pasta cones with ruffles)*
* Fusilli *(corkscrews in various colors and flavors, including wild mushroom and squid ink)*

Pasta Toppings

Offer as many pasta toppings as possible for your guests to choose from. Always use the best-quality and freshest ingredients. Some of these toppings can be sautéed together in extra-virgin olive oil. Others can top the pastas as is. The possibilities are endless.

* Butternut squash, peeled and cut into ½-inch cubes, steamed for 10 minutes with a light sprinkling of coarse salt
* Red onions, peeled and sliced thin, then sautéed over medium-high heat in 1 tablespoon olive oil until translucent
* ½ cup each of fresh thyme, rosemary, sage, and marjoram leaves
* Red tomatoes, seeded and chopped
* Yellow tomatoes, seeded and chopped
* Fresh peas, blanched for 3 minutes, then plunged into ice water
* Swiss chard, finely chopped
* Escarole, cut into 2-inch squares
* Asparagus, cut into 2½-inch lengths, blanched for 3 minutes in boiling water, then plunged into ice water
* Roasted red peppers, seeded and cut into wide strips
* Flat-leaf parsley, stems removed
* Cilantro, stems removed
* Green beans (fino or haricots verts), stems removed and boiled for 3 minutes, then plunged into ice water
* Mint or basil pesto, homemade if possible
* Pine nuts, toasted for 10 minutes in the oven at 350° F.
* Cremini, porcini, and oyster mushrooms, cleaned, stems removed, and cut into large pieces, or left whole if small
* Fresh, skim-milk ricotta cheese
* Fontina cheese, rind removed
* Parmesan cheese, freshly grated
* Gorgonzola cheese, rind scraped off
* Garlic, peeled and finely chopped
* Chives, finely chopped
* Scallions, cleaned and cut into 1-inch pieces
* Sicilian black olives, pitted and sliced
* Italian tomato paste
* Light extra-virgin olive oil
* Coarse salt
* Freshly ground black pepper

Kitchen Tools

These are some kitchen tools and types of equipment that are useful when preparing pasta for a crowd.

* A collection of bowls to hold the pasta toppings. I used bowls from my yellowware collection.
* Two or more pairs of tongs to transfer topping ingredients from the bowls to the pans.
* Nonstick pans, 10 to 14 inches in diameter. I used four so I could keep four pastas going at the same time. For smaller groups, two will do.
* Large plates, forks, and oversized napkins for guests to use on laps. Keep the plates warm in a preheated, turned-off oven or on a plate warmer.
* A cast-iron grill pan with raised ridges in the bottom. When the pan is heated very hot, vegetables, meat, and fish grill nicely and attain those thin brown grill stripes that are so appetizing.
* A rubber spatula to clean the pans after each serving. It is not necessary to wash them each time.

Italian
CORNMEAL CAKE

Serves 20

Simple and crumbly, this cake serves as a nice base for the ricotta ice cream and luscious blood oranges.

2 cups blanched almonds, ground
2 cups yellow cornmeal
½ cup unbleached all-purpose flour
1 cup sugar
1 cup (2 sticks), plus 2 tablespoons unsalted butter, cold

Preheat the oven to 400° F. Butter two 10-inch round pans with removable bottoms.

In a food processor, combine the almonds, cornmeal, flour, and sugar, and process until fine. Add the butter and combine just until the mixture sticks together when pressed between your fingers.

Press the dough evenly into the pans and bake for 20 to 30 minutes, until golden. Allow the cakes to cool in the pans on a rack. Invert them onto plates when cooled; cut into wedges.

Poached Blood
ORANGES

Serves 20

These small oranges are juicy and very flavorful.

¾ cup water
¾ cup dry red wine
¾ cup fresh blood orange juice
¾ cup sugar
20 blood oranges, skin and white membranes carefully peeled

Combine the water, red wine, blood orange juice, and sugar in a large pot. Heat to a simmer and add the oranges.

Poach the oranges over low heat for

10 minutes, and then use a slotted spoon to transfer them to a large bowl.

Increase the heat to high and reduce the poaching liquid by half, about 15 minutes. Serve the liquid poured over the poached oranges. For easy serving, slice the oranges crosswise.

Ricotta
ICE CREAM

Serves 20

This wonderful ice cream does not require an ice cream maker; simply mix it and freeze for an hour.

4 large eggs
⅔ cup sugar
⅔ cup honey
1 tablespoon vanilla extract
2 cups ricotta cheese
2 cups milk
2 cups heavy cream, whipped stiff

In the bowl of an electric mixer, beat the eggs, sugar, and honey until pale yellow in color and tripled in volume, about 5 to 8 minutes.

Stir in the vanilla, ricotta cheese, milk, and whipped heavy cream; continue beating for 2 minutes until smooth and thick. Spread the mixture evenly on a parchment-lined 9 by 13-inch baking sheet and freeze until solid, about 1 hour.

above: *Today, stores sell "fresh" dried pastas in traditional shapes in a wide variety of flavors. For instance, a few years ago stores carried only egg fusilli; then spinach fusilli was introduced, and now even beet and tomato fusilli are available.* **below:** *At certain times of the year blood oranges are in season. These oranges take their name from their dark red flesh and juice. Peeled carefully, with all the membrane removed with a sharp knife, the glistening oranges are poached and served with a generous scoop of the ricotta ice cream and a wedge of the Italian cornmeal cake.*

153

15

Halloween's "GHOULISH" PLEASURES

Serves 12

Pumpkin Pot Pies

✳ Roasted *Leeks* and Wild *Mushrooms*

Watercress–Potato Purée ✳

Chocolate Steamed Pudding

Chocolate Pumpkin Cookies

Halloween's

WHEN I CATERED I WAS OFTEN ASKED AROUND HALLOWEEN TO PREPARE SCARY FEASTS TO CELEBRATE ALLHALLOWS EVE. THIS WAS A CHALLENGE BECAUSE I DID NOT WANT TO FALL INTO THE CATERING CLICHÉS OF "GHOULASH" AND PEELED GRAPES. BUT I DID ALWAYS MAKE SEASONAL FOODS AND DECORATE WITH JACK-O'-LANTERNS AND COBWEBS. THIS HALLOWEEN I RELIED ON PUMPKINS AND SQUASHES FOR MY INSPIRATION: HUGE PUMPKINS AND MEDIUM PUMPKINS CUT OUT AND CARVED INTO JACK-O'-LANTERNS WITH UNIQUE FACES AND PATTERNS, AND SMALL SUGAR PUMPKINS FOR DELICIOUS PASTRY-COVERED POT PIES FILLED WITH SAVORY CORNISH HENS. I MAINTAINED A BLACK AND ORANGE THEME FOR THE DECORATIONS AND TABLE SETTINGS, COVERING THE TABLE WITH AN INGRAIN CARPET OF BRIGHT RED AND ORANGE HUES. I USED BLACK COLOMBIAN CLAY DISHES, BLACK PAINTED GRANGE CHAIRS, DARK GREENISH-BLACK NAPKINS, AND GOBLETS OF DEEPEST AMETHYST AND CITRON YELLOW. I NEVER ASK GUESTS TO DRESS IN COSTUME FOR THIS TYPE OF HALLOWEEN DINNER. INSTEAD, THE DECORATIONS AND THE FOODS CREATE THE MOOD. BUT COSTUMES, IF YOU WISH, WOULD CERTAINLY ENHANCE THE PARTY AND ADD TO THE FUN. JUST REMEMBER TO TURN DOWN THE LIGHTS, STIR UP THE DRY ICE FOR LOTS OF EERIE "MIST" AND "SMOKE," AND PLAY SPOOKY MUSIC.

previous page: *Pulled from the ceiling rafters to the table and the chairs were the "instant cobwebs" one can buy in craft stores; the white filament created perfect filigreed spiders' webs. The center of the table was mounded with all the littlest gourds and pumpkins I could find.* above: *Pumpkins were once only carved with jagged teeth and triangle eyes. Now, using carving tools and a sculptor's vision, pumpkins of all sizes are transformed into architecture, designs, faces, and caricatures. By only cutting partially through the thick pumpkin wall you can create varying degrees of transparency and opaqueness.*

above: *Sugar pumpkins are filled with chunks of herb-roasted Cornish hens, along with a medley of vegetables.* below: *Puff pastry was rolled into rounds about two inches bigger than the pumpkin opening. An egg wash was used like glue to affix the pastry to the pumpkin. Decorative pastry cutouts of pumpkin leaves and vine tendrils were "glued" with more egg wash to the pastry top, and then the entire surface was glazed again. Cut a small hole in each pastry cap to allow steam to escape from the cavity while baking.*

Pumpkin POT PIES

Serves 12

The meat from herb-roasted Cornish hens, fresh-cooked vegetables, and a delicately flavored sauce fill the cavity of each sugar pumpkin for a delicious variation on the pot pie.

- 1 tablespoon unsalted butter
- 6 garlic cloves, minced
- 6 1½-pound Cornish game hens
- 1 lemon, thinly sliced
- 1 bunch fresh thyme
- 1 bunch fresh rosemary
- 1 bunch fresh sage
- 1 bunch fresh basil
- 1 bunch fresh parsley
  Salt and freshly ground pepper
- 6 cups chicken stock
- 1 bottle dry vermouth or dry white wine
- 6 carrots, peeled and cut in chunks
- 4 leeks, cut up
- 4 stalks celery, chopped
- 4 medium white turnips, peeled and quartered
- 6 parsnips, peeled and quartered
- 2 pounds carrots, peeled and cut in 1-inch pieces
- 1 acorn squash, peeled, seeded, and cut in wedges
- ½ pound white pearl onions
- ½ pound yellow pearl onions
- ½ pound haricots verts
- 12 3-pound pumpkins
- 6 pounds homemade puff pastry (see Note), or 6 1-pound boxes (12 sheets) frozen prepared puff pastry, thawed
  Pot Pie Sauce (recipe follows)
- 2 large eggs, lightly beaten

In a small sauté pan, melt the butter over medium-high heat. Add the minced garlic and sauté briefly, just until it becomes fragrant. Remove from heat and set aside.

Fill the cavity of each hen with a slice of lemon, some of the sautéed garlic, 2 sprigs of thyme, 1 sprig of rosemary, 1 sage leaf, 2 basil leaves, 2 sprigs of parsley, and salt and pepper. Place the hens in a deep casserole. Cover with the chicken stock, wine, 6 carrots, leeks, and celery, and poach, covered, over medium heat for 40 to 50 minutes, until tender. Let stand in the broth for an additional 10 to 15 minutes. Allow to cool, then remove the meat from the bones in large chunks, discarding the bones, skin, and herbs.

Reduce the cooking liquid by boiling over high heat until it is reduced to 4 cups. Strain and reserve to make the Pot Pie Sauce.

Meanwhile, in a large stockpot, bring 1 inch of water to a boil. Add the turnips, parsnips, 2 pounds of carrots, and squash, and cook, covered, over medium-high heat until tender, about 12 to 15 minutes.

Using a paring knife, make an X on the bottom of each onion. Place in a saucepan with just enough water to cover, bring to a boil, and cook for 5 to 10 minutes. Drain. When cool enough to handle, peel; the skins will slip right off.

Bring water to a boil in a small saucepan. Add the haricots verts, cover the pot, and cook just until tender, about 5 minutes. Drain.

Wash the pumpkins well and cut off the top quarter of each, creating an opening about 8 inches in diameter. Reserve the tops. With a spoon, remove the seeds and stringy fibers from both top and bottom.

Preheat the oven to 450° F. Roll the dough on a floured surface to ⅛ inch thick, and with a paring knife cut 12 circles approximately 10 inches in diameter; reserve excess pastry.

After baking, the pastry caps are gorgeous, puffed and golden brown. One pumpkin serves one guest; serve piping hot with Watercress-Potato Purée for a delicious and memorable Halloween meal.

Fill each pumpkin with the meat of half a hen, dividing white and dark meat evenly. Divide the onions, haricots, and turnip-parsnip medley evenly among the pumpkins. Ladle equal amounts of the Pot Pie Sauce over the fillings. Brush the rim of each pumpkin with the lightly beaten egg wash and place a circular piece of pastry over the top, gently pressing the pastry around the rim of the pumpkin to make it adhere.

Decorate the pastry caps with leaves made from the pastry scraps. Brush the pastry with the beaten egg. Cut a small vent in each pastry cap. Place the stuffed pumpkins and the pumpkin tops on baking sheets lined with parchment paper. Bake for 15 minutes, then reduce the heat to 350° for 10 to 15 minutes. Turn off the oven and keep the pumpkins there for 5 minutes.

Serve piping hot, with pumpkin tops as garnish.

Note: I always use homemade puff pastry, although prepared pastry can now be purchased. The recipe I use is in Pies & Tarts.

Pot Pie Sauce

Makes 4 ½ cups

- 8 tablespoons (1 stick) unsalted butter
- 8 tablespoons unbleached all-purpose flour
- 4 cups reduced stock
- 1½ cups heavy cream
- 3 tablespoons cognac
  Salt and freshly ground pepper
  Fresh lemon juice

In a large, shallow pan melt the butter over medium-low heat. Mix in the flour gradually, whisking constantly. Cook until smooth, about 3 minutes. Stir in the reduced stock, whisking to break up lumps. Add the heavy cream, cognac, and salt and pepper to taste. Bring the mixture to a gentle boil over medium-high heat. Cook until it thickens, about 5 minutes. Add several drops of lemon juice to taste.

Keep the sauce warm at the back of the stove until ready to use, or refrigerate with a piece of plastic wrap placed directly on the surface to prevent a skin from forming.

Poaching the leeks for a few minutes before transferring them to the oven for roasting ensures a tasty and delicate tenderness.

Roasted LEEKS and Wild MUSHROOMS

Serves 12

Fresh blackfoot mushrooms add just the correct amount of woodsy darkness to the well-roasted leeks.

- 12–16 large leeks, roots trimmed
- ½ cup (1 stick) unsalted butter
- 1 cup water
  Salt and freshly ground pepper
- ½ pound whole fresh blackfoot mushrooms
- 2 tablespoons chopped fresh parsley
- 1 tablespoon balsamic vinegar
- 3 tablespoons extra-virgin olive oil

Preheat the oven to 450° F.

Cut the leeks to a uniform length of 7 to 8 inches, making sure to cut only the green ends. Slice the leeks in half lengthwise, starting 1 inch up from the root end.

Wash the leeks thoroughly, separating the leaves under cold running water to remove sand.

In a large saucepan, melt ¼ cup of the butter in the water. Add salt, pepper, and the leeks and poach over medium heat for 5 to 8 minutes, until tender. Drain the leeks. Arrange the leeks in a single layer in a large roasting pan and roast for 30 minutes.

Meanwhile, melt the remaining ¼ cup butter in a skillet. Add the mushrooms and the chopped parsley and sauté for 2 to 3 minutes. Add salt and pepper to taste.

In a mixing bowl, whisk together the balsamic vinegar and olive oil.

Slice each leek into fourths and place one leek on each plate. Garnish with several wild mushrooms and drizzle with the balsamic vinaigrette.

WATERCRESS-POTATO Purée

Serves 12

Containing two favorites—potatoes and watercress—this purée is an ideal side dish.

- 8 large Idaho potatoes, peeled and quartered
- 2 bunches watercress, tough stems removed
- 4 tablespoons extra-virgin olive oil

¼ cup (½ stick) unsalted butter, melted

¼ cup heavy cream

Salt and freshly ground pepper

Preheat the oven to 500° F., and line a baking sheet with a piece of parchment paper.

Place the potatoes in a large saucepan with cold water to cover. Bring to a boil and cook until tender, about 25 minutes. Drain, then place the potatoes on the baking sheet and dry them in the oven for 10 minutes. Pass the potatoes through a ricer or mash them by hand.

Blanch the watercress in boiling water for 3 minutes or until bright green. Drain, then immediately plunge the watercress into a bowl of ice water to set the color. Drain again and transfer to a blender or food processor; purée while adding the olive oil.

In a large bowl, whip the mashed potatoes with the watercress purée, melted butter, heavy cream, and salt and pepper to taste until well combined. Reheat the mixture over low heat and serve.

above: *The roasted leeks with wild mushrooms can be served either as a first course on separate small plates as pictured here, or alongside the savory Pumpkin Pot Pies with the Watercress-Potato Purée.* right: *I roasted the tops of each pumpkin as well as the pot pies, and they looked quite lovely garnishing each plate.*

Halloween

Chocolate Steamed PUDDING

Serves 10 to 12

You can serve this delicious dessert either warm or at room temperature.

5 tablespoons unsalted butter
13 tablespoons sugar
1½ cups light cream
½ vanilla bean or 1 teaspoon
   vanilla extract
5 ounces semisweet chocolate,
   cut into small pieces
2 tablespoons unbleached
   all-purpose flour
5 eggs, separated
2 tablespoons dark rum or brandy
   Confectioners' sugar
   Squash vines or ivy

Use 2 tablespoons of the butter to generously butter a 1-quart metal pudding mold, including the inside of the lid. Add 3 tablespoons of the sugar, replace the lid tightly, and shake vigorously. Remove the lid and discard any excess sugar.

Put the cream into a small heavy saucepan and add the vanilla bean or extract and the chocolate pieces. Cook over low heat, stirring occasionally, for 5 to 10 minutes or until the chocolate is melted. Set aside.

Melt the remaining butter in another small saucepan and add the flour. Cook over low heat about 1 minute, until blended. Stirring continuously, slowly add the cream and chocolate mixture. Cook over low heat for 5 to 8 minutes, stirring until thickened. Remove the vanilla bean.

Place the egg yolks and the remaining sugar into a large mixing bowl. Beat until thick and lemon-colored. Slowly beat in the warm chocolate mixture. Add the liquor and mix well.

We made whimsical chocolate cookie pumpkins and spread them with orange icing and green trim. Everyone loved these cookies.

In the bowl of an electric mixer, beat the egg whites until they are stiff. Beat 4 tablespoons of the egg whites into the chocolate mixture. Gently, but thoroughly, fold in the remaining egg whites. Carefully pour the pudding into the prepared mold and place the lid on securely. Place the mold on a rack in a large stockpot filled with enough water to come halfway up the sides of the mold. Simmer, covered, over low heat for 1 hour and 15 minutes.

Remove the pudding mold from the pot and allow to cool for 5 to 10 minutes. To unmold the pudding, remove the lid and run a knife around the edge of the pudding while it is still warm. Carefully invert it onto a serving plate. If it sticks, gently tap the mold with a wooden spoon. Allow the pudding to cool completely and sprinkle it with confectioners' sugar. Arrange squash vines or ivy around the pudding for decoration.

Chocolate Pumpkin COOKIES

Makes 4 dozen

Create a pumpkin-shaped cardboard stencil 5 to 6 inches in diameter to make these cookies.

1½ cups (3 sticks) unsalted butter
1¾ cups sugar
2 large eggs, lightly beaten
3 cups unbleached all-purpose
   flour
1½ cups cocoa
¼ teaspoon salt
⅓ teaspoon freshly ground pepper
1 teaspoon ground cinnamon
   Orange and green Simple
   Cookie Icing (page 52)

In a mixing bowl, cream together the butter and sugar. Add the eggs, one at a time, incorporating them thoroughly, then beat until fluffy.

In another bowl, sift together the flour, cocoa, salt, pepper, and cinnamon. Add to the butter mixture gradually, beating until well incorporated. If the mixture seems soft, add more flour. Divide the dough into thirds and wrap each third as a flat round in plastic wrap. Chill for 1 hour.

Heat the oven to 375° F. Butter a cookie sheet.

On a well-floured board, roll out the dough to ⅛ inch thick. Using a cardboard stencil and a sharp knife, cut out pumpkin shapes. Transfer the cookies to the baking sheet, spacing them ½ inch apart. Bake until crisp but not darkened, about 8 to 10 minutes. Transfer to a rack and cool before icing. Spread the cookies with orange icing, then put the green icing in a pastry bag fitted with a small circular tip and use to create trim and design.

left: *Corey Tippin carved this face for me—it's scary, translucent, and very effective in the dark with a candle burning inside. A good trick: cut out the bottom of the pumpkin so that you fit the shell over the lighted candle. This avoids lots of burnt fingers.* **right**: *A variety of pumpkins create the appropriate seasonal feeling.*

right: *A very popular and delectable dessert is a steamed chocolate pudding; it is so light, and yet tastes of the essence of good chocolate. I steamed this pudding in a melon mold and decorated it with squash vines and blossoms.*

above left: *Hobnail goblets of deep purple contrasted nicely with delicate citron glasses.* **right**: *Tin melon molds come in various sizes. You can find them in gourmet cooking stores. Try to buy good-quality, heavy tin-coated metal.*

16

Thanksgiving at Turkey HILL

Serves 10

Sweet Potato and *Apple* Soup ✱ Basil and Thyme Toast

Kathy's *Endive-Apple* Salad ✱ Roast *Turkey* with Mosaic of Sage

Orzo and *Porcini* Stuffing ✱ Simple *Cornbread* Dressing

Fresh Cranberry Sauce ✱ Sautéed *Red Cabbage* in Red Wine

Sautéed *Spinach* with Garlic

Steamed Purple *Broccoli* and *Cauliflower*

Fresh *Pea* and Apple Purée ✱ *Beet* and Balsamic Vinegar Purée

Turnip and *Pear* Purée ✱ Cranberry-Currant Spice Cake

Baked Apple *Tart* ✱ *Sautéed* Apple Tart

Thanksgiving

EVERY YEAR I THINK THAT I WILL DINE ELSEWHERE ON THANKSGIVING DAY—
THAT FOR ONCE I WILL NOT STUFF MYRIAD TURKEYS, CRUSH POUNDS OF CRANBER-
RIES, AND PURÉE UNTOLD VARIETIES OF VEGETABLES. YET THE TRADITION OF THE
HOLIDAY IS SO MUCH A PART OF WHAT I DO, WHAT I LIVE FOR, THAT TO NOT COOK
AND ENTERTAIN ON THIS DAY WOULD SEEM TANTAMOUNT TO TREASON. AND SO WE
ALWAYS END UP HAVING OUR TRADITIONAL FAMILY DINNER AT MY HOUSE.
NEVERTHELESS, I HAVE TRIED TO SIMPLIFY MY EFFORTS, AND I HAVE CUT DOWN ON
THE NUMBER OF DISHES THAT I PREPARE FOR THIS BOUNTIFUL CELEBRATION.
ALTHOUGH I LIKE TO VARY EACH PREPARATION, I TRY TO KEEP WITHIN THE CON-
FINES OF A NEW ENGLAND THANKSGIVING IN TERMS OF THE INGREDIENTS I USE: I
HAVE NOT YET RESORTED TO BARBECUED TURKEY, OR TO BLUE CORN TORTILLA
SOUP AS A STARTER. FOR THIS MENU I PUT THE SWEET POTATOES IN A SOUP, AND A
LOT OF SPICES IN THE CAKE. PEARS AND APPLES FLAVOR THE VEGETABLE PURÉES,
SWEETENING THEM AND MAKING THEM EXCEEDINGLY PALATABLE TO EVERYONE'S
TASTE. A NEW STUFFING, MADE WITH ORZO AND PORCINI MUSHROOMS, WAS INSPIRED
BY MY FRIEND DORA FERREYRA, WHO WAS COOKING WITH LEFTOVERS ONE DAY AND
PUT ORZO, INSTEAD OF BREAD, IN HER STUFFING. IT WAS, AND IS, SIMPLY DELICIOUS.

left: *I covered the dining table with an old quilt woven of very strong cotton. It has survived many years of laundering and pressing.* right: *I used napkins made from linen toweling, white striped with blue.*

right: *I found the cobalt-striped Paris porcelain tureen monogrammed with a large S at what was then the Starring Mansion, a hilltop home with a windmill and gardens and views all the way to New York City. The heirs decided to "tag sale" the entire house, and I was lucky enough to buy the tureens and vegetable dishes of the extensive dinner set.*

previous page: *A few years ago I found these amazing cobalt-blue and white turkey dishes and platters in an antique shop. They were made in Germany, by the Meissen porcelain works. I don't know their age, but the color and the hand of the artist make them very special to me.*

above left: *I discovered this flat-ware at the Rose d'Or consignment shop in Darien, Connecticut. Wild boars and beasts are stylized into the handles.* right: *These placecards were in an old box I bought. They were inscribed with different names, one of which was Martha. I use them every Thanksgiving, even if the names don't fit the guests.*

Because I had decided on a blue and white theme this year, I used all of the Leeds creamware (circa 1800) from my closet. Much of it was collected from a local dealer, Pat Guthman, although I've picked up a piece or two at tag sales and shops. This blue feather-edged tableware goes well with the Meissen, and even with the Paris porcelain. We ate in the barn, where a leather-topped Mission table doubled as a buffet. The turkey was surrounded by the sautéed red cabbage and the sautéed fresh spinach, with the endive-apple salad and the broccoli and cauliflower alongside it.

Sweet Potato and APPLE SOUP

Serves 10

This soup is a delightfully different way to include sweet potatoes in your holiday menu.

1 tablespoon unsalted butter
1 large onion, peeled and diced
2 shallots, peeled and minced
2 pounds sweet potatoes, peeled and cut in cubes
½ pound carrots, peeled and cut in cubes
2 tart apples, peeled, cored, and cut in cubes
½ ripe papaya, peeled, seeded, and cut in cubes
3 cups chicken stock
1 cup water
½ cup crème fraîche (page 40)
½ bunch fresh thyme

Melt the butter in a large stockpot. Add the onion and shallots and sauté over medium-high heat for 3 to 5 minutes. Reduce the heat, add the sweet potatoes, carrots, apples, and papaya, and continue to sauté for an additional 8 minutes, stirring frequently.

Add the chicken stock and water. Simmer for 30 minutes or until the vegetables and fruits are soft.

Transfer the soup to a food processor in batches and purée. Return the soup to a saucepan, blend well, and reheat if necessary. Thin with a bit more stock if the soup is too thick. Serve the soup hot, garnished with a dollop of crème fraîche and a sprig of fresh thyme.

Garnished with fresh thyme and crème fraîche, the sweet potato and apple soup was very satisfying.

Basil and Thyme TOAST

Serves 10

Crisp and flavorful toast always disappears quickly.

3 tablespoons unsalted butter, melted, or extra-virgin olive oil
3 tablespoons finely chopped fresh basil
1½ tablespoons finely chopped fresh thyme
1 loaf brioche or Italian bread, sliced thin

Preheat the broiler to 500° F.

In a bowl, combine the butter, basil, and thyme.

Cut the bread slices in half. Toast the bread under the broiler for about 1 to 2 minutes per side, until crisp and just turning golden. Remove and brush with the herbed butter. Place under the broiler for an additional 1 to 2 minutes until golden brown. Serve immediately.

Kathy's ENDIVE-APPLE SALAD

Serves 10

You will enjoy the lovely contrast of tastes and textures in this salad—sweet and tart, smooth and crunchy.

½ cup whole walnuts
7 Belgian endives, bottoms trimmed
1 tablespoon honey
1 tablespoon Dijon mustard
¼ cup rice vinegar
3 tablespoons extra-virgin olive oil
½ teaspoon walnut oil
Salt and freshly ground pepper
2 tart apples, such as Rome or McIntosh, cored and diced
½ cup pomegranate seeds (optional)

Preheat the oven to 300° F.

Place the walnuts on a baking sheet and toast in the oven for 3 to 5 minutes. Watch closely after 2 minutes because they brown quickly. Cool the walnuts, then chop coarsely and set aside.

Remove the large outer leaves of the endives and reserve them, discarding any that are bruised or wilted. Slice the remaining endives on the diagonal.

In a small bowl, whisk together the honey, mustard, rice vinegar, olive oil, and walnut oil. Add salt and pepper to taste.

Arrange the reserved endive leaves around the edge of a platter. In a large bowl, toss the sliced endives, the apples, and the walnuts with the dressing to combine. Spoon the salad into the center of the platter and sprinkle with the pomegranate seeds.

Thanksgiving

ROAST TURKEY
with Mosaic of SAGE

Serves 10

Try to find an organically grown, free-range, corn-fed turkey. The flesh is very tender, and the cooking time is reduced.

1 26-pound fresh turkey
1 tablespoon extra-virgin olive oil
20 fresh sage leaves
   Coarse salt
   Orzo and Porcini Stuffing
   (recipe follows)
1 cup (2 sticks) unsalted butter, melted for basting
2 cups dry vermouth

Preheat the oven to 350° F.

Remove the neck and gizzards from inside the turkey and rinse the bird thoroughly with cold water. Pat dry. Rub the olive oil over the entire surface of the turkey. Using your fingers, gently loosen the skin of the turkey from the breast and drumsticks. Carefully arrange individual leaves of sage under the skin in a mosaic pattern. Lightly salt the cavity.

Stuff the turkey loosely with the stuffing and truss it. Place it on a rack in a large roasting pan lined with aluminum foil and generously brush with melted butter. Roast the turkey, basting every 30 minutes with melted butter and pan juices, for 6 to 6½ hours, or until an instant-read thermometer inserted in the thigh registers 180° F. During the last half hour, add the dry vermouth to the pan. If the turkey legs or breast brown too quickly, cover them lightly with foil.

Transfer the turkey to a cutting board, reserving the pan juices for gravy. Remove the stuffing, tent the turkey with foil, and allow it to sit for 20 to 30 minutes before carving.

Orzo and Porcini STUFFING

Makes enough for a 26-pound turkey

The variations possible for turkey stuffings are endless, but this one is particularly delicious.

1 loaf French bread, thinly sliced
2–3 cups chicken stock
½ pound orzo
2 tablespoons extra-virgin olive oil
4 fresh large porcini mushrooms, or ½ cup dried, plumped in warm water
4 tablespoons (½ stick) unsalted butter
3 large onions, peeled and coarsely chopped
3 shallots, peeled and chopped
6 celery stalks, chopped, leaves included
1 red bell pepper, seeded and diced
1 tablespoon dried oregano
2 tablespoons chopped fresh parsley
   Salt and freshly ground pepper

Preheat the oven to 300° F.

Arrange the bread slices on a baking sheet and bake until lightly browned and dry, about 10 minutes. Allow the bread to cool slightly, then transfer to a food processor to create fine crumbs.

In a large saucepan, bring the chicken stock to a boil. Add the orzo and cook over high heat, stirring occasionally, for 8 to 10 minutes, until tender. Drain, reserving the stock. Toss the orzo with the olive oil and set aside.

Clean the mushrooms, trim the bottoms of the stems, and chop. Melt the butter in a large sauté pan. Add the onions and shallots and sauté over medium-high heat for 5 minutes. Add the mushrooms, celery, red pepper, and oregano, and continue sautéing

for about 4 minutes, or until the mushrooms are just tender.

In a large mixing bowl, gently stir together the bread crumbs, orzo, sautéed vegetables, and parsley. If necessary add some of the reserved stock to moisten the stuffing. Season with salt and pepper.

Simple Cornbread DRESSING

Serves 10

Of course, there can never be enough stuffing at Thanksgiving, so make plenty of extra.

3 tablespoons unsalted butter
1 large onion, chopped
2 shallots, peeled and chopped
4 celery stalks, diced
1 large egg, lightly beaten
1 cup chicken stock
4 cups cornbread, crumbled
1 tablespoon fresh thyme
½ cup chopped fresh parsley
   Salt and freshly ground pepper

Preheat the oven to 350° F.

Melt the butter in a large skillet. Add the onion, shallots, and celery and sauté over medium-high heat for 5 minutes, until softened.

In a large bowl, whisk together the egg and chicken stock. Add the crumbled cornbread, sautéed vegetables, thyme, parsley, and salt and pepper to taste. Toss until well combined. Place in a buttered 9 by 13-inch ovenproof baking dish and bake uncovered for 30 minutes or until golden brown.

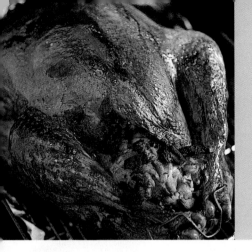

left: *The turkey was a freshly killed bird, one of the large broad-breasted whites that I raise each year for the occasion. I always loosen the skin and insert herbs underneath for additional flavor.* below: *The food looked especially colorful on the Meissen plates. I found the plaid tablecloth fabric in Amsterdam's famous flea market.*

above: *I served the fresh cranberry sauce in a handsome Leeds tureen.*
below: *The three vegetable and fruit purées—red beet and balsamic vinegar, green pea and apple, and white turnip with pear—are delicious whether served alone or presented together on a big platter to create a colorful sampling.*

Fresh CRANBERRY SAUCE

Serves 10

For this sauce, I like the berries tart, stewed with a small amount of sugar just until they pop.

 4 cups fresh cranberries
 ½ cup sugar
 ¼ cup water
    Juice of 1 orange

Rinse the cranberries well and discard any that are soft or bruised.

In a large saucepan, combine the cranberries with the sugar, water, and orange juice. Bring to a boil over medium-high heat, stirring often.

Reduce to a gentle boil and cook the berries, uncovered, just until they pop, about 10 minutes. Chill.

Sautéed RED CABBAGE in Red Wine

Serves 10

Red wine and wine vinegar impart to the cabbage a tart, full flavor.

 3 tablespoons unsalted butter
 1 large onion, thinly sliced
 1 large head red cabbage, shredded
    Zest of 2 oranges
 1 teaspoon sugar
 ½ cup dry red wine
 ½ cup red wine vinegar
    Salt and freshly ground pepper

Melt the butter in a large sauté pan. Add the onion and sauté over medium-high heat until transparent, about 5 minutes.

Add the cabbage, orange zest, sugar, red wine, vinegar, and salt and pepper to taste and mix well. Lower the heat to medium and cook for an additional 15 minutes, stirring occasionally, until the cabbage is wilted.

Sautéed SPINACH with Garlic

Serves 10

Remember this simple dish through-out the year, whenever you need a quick vegetable.

 2 pounds spinach
 1 tablespoon extra-virgin olive oil
 3 garlic cloves, sliced
    Salt and freshly ground pepper

Wash the spinach thoroughly in several changes of water. Discard the tough stems.

Heat the oil in a large sauté pan and sauté the garlic over medium-high heat for 1 minute. Add the spinach and sauté for 3 minutes, tossing constantly until just wilted. Season with salt and pepper.

Steamed PURPLE BROCCOLI and Cauliflower

Serves 10

Green broccoli can also be used, although the purple makes an attractive color contrast with the cauliflower.

 2 heads purple broccoli
 2 heads cauliflower
 2 tablespoons unsalted butter
 3 tablespoons bread crumbs

Trim the leaves from the broccoli and cut into large flowerets. Leave the green neatly trimmed around the bottom of the cauliflower. Cut the stalk so the cauliflower will stand upright, and make a large X in the bottom of each stalk to shorten cooking time.

Bring 2 large saucepans of water to a boil. In one pan steam the broccoli, covered, over medium heat until just tender, about 10 minutes. Steam the cauliflower in the other pan one at a time, covered, over medium heat, for 10 to 15 minutes, until tender when pricked with a knife.

In a skillet, melt the butter and add the bread crumbs. Brown slightly. Arrange the broccoli side by side with the cauliflower on a large platter and sprinkle with the buttered crumbs. Serve hot.

An early handpainted tole vase was filled with autumnal flowers—'Love-Lies-Bleeding' and sedum 'Autumn Joy'.

FRESH PEA *and* APPLE *Purée*

Serves 10

Frozen peas work equally well as fresh in this purée.

- 1½ pounds fresh shelled peas, or 3 10-ounce boxes frozen
- 4 tablespoons (½ stick) unsalted butter
- 1 onion, finely minced
- 2 tart apples, such as Rome or McIntosh, peeled and quartered

Steam the peas in a vegetable steamer over simmering water for about 6 to 8 minutes until tender (less if using frozen peas).

In a medium skillet, melt the butter. Add the onion and apples and sauté over medium-high heat until very tender, about 8 minutes.

Combine the peas, onion, and apples in a food processor and purée until smooth. Return the purée to a saucepan and rewarm gently over very low heat.

BEET *and* BALSAMIC VINEGAR *Purée*

Serves 10

Placing the roasted beets on a piece of parchment paper will prevent your work surface from discoloring. Wear rubber gloves to protect your hands.

- 2½ pounds beets, roots and stems trimmed
- 1 tablespoon balsamic vinegar
- ¼ cup (½ stick) unsalted butter, cut in pieces
  Salt and freshly ground pepper

Preheat the oven to 400° F. Wrap the beets in aluminum foil, and roast for 2 hours or until tender when pricked with a knife. Allow them to cool enough to handle, then slip off the skins. Cut the beets in quarters.

Transfer the beets to a food processor, add the balsamic vinegar, butter, and salt and pepper to taste, and purée until smooth. Return the purée to a saucepan and reheat gently over very low heat.

TURNIP *and* PEAR *Purée*

Serves 10

I sometimes add heavy cream to this purée to enhance its consistency, but it is even delicious without. Make sure your pears are ripe and tender.

- 2½ pounds white turnips, peeled and quartered
- ½ cup (1 stick) unsalted butter
- 1 onion, finely chopped
- 2 pears, peeled, cored, and diced
- ¼ cup heavy cream (optional)
  Salt and freshly ground pepper

In a large saucepan, place the turnips on a rack over boiling water. Steam, covered, for 20 to 25 minutes, until tender when pricked with a knife. Remove from the heat.

In a small skillet, melt the butter. Add the onion and sauté over medium heat until translucent, about 4 to 5 minutes. Add the pears and sauté until tender, about 5 minutes.

Combine the turnips, pears, and onion in a food processor and purée until smooth (you may need to work in batches).

Return the purée to a saucepan and reheat over very low heat. Add the heavy cream if desired, stirring thoroughly until combined. Season with salt and pepper to taste.

Thanksgiving

Cranberry-Currant
SPICE CAKE

Serves 10

I have made different versions of this cake ever since I was in junior high school.

2⅓ cups cake flour, sifted twice before measuring
1½ teaspoons baking powder
½ teaspoon baking soda
1 teaspoon freshly grated nutmeg
1 teaspoon cinnamon
½ teaspoon ground cloves
¼ teaspoon ground ginger
¼ teaspoon ground allspice
½ teaspoon salt
¾ cup (1½ sticks) unsalted butter
1½ cups sugar, sifted
3 large eggs, separated
1 cup buttermilk or ½ cup buttermilk and ½ cup applesauce
⅓ pound dried cranberries
¼ pound dried currants

Preheat the oven to 350° F. Butter and flour a 9-inch tube cake pan.

Sift the cake flour with the baking powder, baking soda, nutmeg, cinnamon, cloves, ginger, allspice, and salt.

In a separate bowl cream the butter with the sugar until fluffy. Beat in the egg yolks, one at a time, mixing well after each addition, until light and creamy. Stir in the flour mixture in thirds, alternating with the buttermilk. Stir in the dried cranberries and currants.

In the bowl of an electric mixer, whip the egg whites until stiff but not dry and fold into the cake batter. Pour the batter into the prepared cake pan and bake for 1 hour or until a cake tester inserted into the center of the cake comes out clean. Turn out on a rack to cool.

Baked
APPLE TART

Serves 10

The apple jelly makes a well-flavored glaze for this classic dessert tart.

Sugar Crust

2 cups unbleached all-purpose flour
1 cup confectioners' sugar
¾ cup (1½ sticks) unsalted butter, chilled and cut in pieces
¼ teaspoon salt
2 large eggs

Filling

9 Gala apples, peeled and cored
¾ cup sugar
1 tablespoon ground cinnamon

½ cup apple jelly

To make the sugar crust, in a food processor, combine the flour, sugar, butter, and salt and process for 15 to 20 seconds, until the mixture resembles coarse oatmeal. Add the eggs one at a time and process for 20 seconds, until the dough just holds together.

Press the dough into an 11-inch tart pan with a removable bottom. Wrap in plastic wrap and chill for 1 hour in the refrigerator.

Preheat the oven to 350° F.

Remove the plastic wrap and cover the shell with aluminum foil. Fill the pan with pie weights or dried beans; this helps retain the shape of the crust while baking. Bake the crust for 18 minutes, then remove the foil and weights and bake until golden brown, about 7 minutes longer. Allow to cool before adding the filling.

To make the filling, cut the apples into eighths, then toss in a mixing bowl

with the sugar and cinnamon. Mound in the prebaked pie shell and bake for 35 minutes. Do not overbake or the apples will collapse. Transfer the pie to a rack to cool thoroughly.

Right before serving, heat the apple jelly in a small saucepan over low heat until melted. Remove the ring from the tart pan and brush the top of the tart with the melted apple jelly.

Sautéed
APPLE TART

Serves 10

Sautéing rather than baking these apples produces a delectable tart with tender yet firm fruit.

9 Gala or Granny Smith apples, cored and peeled
4 tablespoons (½ stick) unsalted butter
¾ cup sugar
1 teaspoon cinnamon
½ cup cranberry jelly
1 Sugar Crust (recipe precedes), prebaked and cooled

Preheat the oven to 350° F. Cut the apples into eighths.

In a large skillet, melt the butter. Add the apples, sugar, and cinnamon and sauté over medium heat until the apples are just tender and caramelized, about 8 to 10 minutes. Transfer the apples to a bowl, using a slotted spoon. Add the cranberry jelly to the skillet and continue to cook for 3 to 5 minutes, until the sauce is reduced to a syrupy glaze.

Arrange the apples in a neat circular pattern in the prebaked pie shell. Strain the syrup through a sieve, drizzling over the tart.

clockwise from top left: *The Cranberry-Currant Spice Cake was studded with dried cranberries and raisins; I used the only other blue and white plates I had—diner plates from the fifties with a painted blue edge. Apple tarts made from sautéed apples will hold their shape, whereas apple slices baked to a similar tenderness will be much softer. I've included the recipes for both; the sautéed version is on the top right. I grow many apples in my orchard and always save a large basket of them in the cold cellar for use at Thanksgiving time. The tart on the bottom left uses baked apples.*

17

HOLIDAY Dessert *Buffet*

Serves 25

✴ Baked Gala *Apples*

Chocolate Devil's Food Cake with Seven-Minute Frosting

Yellow Pound Cake with *Blood Orange* Glaze

Lemon-Glazed Pound Cake with *Candied Kumquats*

Steamed *Persimmon* Pudding with Persimmon Purée

Steamed *Ginger* Pudding ✴

Steamed *Brioche* Pudding with Sour Lemon Cream Sauce

✴ *Bûche de Noël*

HOLIDAY Dessert *Buffet*

IT IS QUITE A CHALLENGE TO COME UP WITH NEW IDEAS FOR CHRISTMAS ENTER-
TAINING YEAR AFTER YEAR. I'VE HAD BUFFET DINNERS, SIT-DOWN DINNERS, COCK-
TAIL PARTIES, HORS D'OEUVRES AND DESSERT PARTIES, AND EGGNOG AND COOKIES
PARTIES. LAST YEAR I HAD JUST DESSERTS. I'VE LONG BEEN FASCINATED WITH
"SHAPELY" CAKES, AND AFTER ASSEMBLING ALL MY LARGE, PRETTY MOLDS, I
MATCHED SOME OF MY FAVORITE STEAMED PUDDING AND CAKE RECIPES TO THE
VARIOUS PANS AND MOLDS. I WANTED THE ENTIRE PARTY TO HAVE A COUNTRY
FEELING, SO I SET UP THE MAJORITY OF THE DESSERTS IN THE KITCHEN.
ELSEWHERE I LAID OUT PLATES OF COOKIES, AND IN THE DINING ROOM I SET OUT A
MASSIVE SILVER TRAY WITH AN APPROPRIATELY WINTRY-LOOKING BUCHE DE NOEL.
HOT MULLED WHITE WINE WAS SERVED FROM HUGE EARTHENWARE BOWLS. OVER
THE YEARS I'VE COLLECTED MANY CUT-GLASS AND PRESSED-GLASS PUNCH CUPS,
AND I ARRANGED THESE AROUND THE BOWLS OF HOT WINE. IN ADDITION TO
THE WINE I OFFERED A CHOICE OF CAFFE LATTE, HOT LEMON TEA, MINERAL
WATERS, AND CHAMPAGNE. IT WAS A SUCCESSFUL VARIATION ON THE USUAL HOLI-
DAY PARTY: ALTHOUGH THE ASSORTMENT OF DESSERTS WAS IMPRESSIVE, THESE
BEAUTIFULLY FORMED CONFECTIONS WERE ALL QUITE EASY TO MAKE.

previous page: *I'm convinced that a splendid dessert array is one of the most tempting sights imaginable! Clockwise from left, the buffet included a steamed persimmon pudding with persimmon purée, a yellow pound cake with blood orange glaze, a steamed ginger pudding, and a pound cake with lemon syrup and candied kumquats.* above: *The yellow pound cake with blood orange glaze looks particularly appetizing atop my favorite colored cake stand, an amethyst Depression glass stand from the thirties.*

Baked Gala APPLES

Makes 8 apples

These are great served with a pitcher of heavy cream, softly whipped cream, or crème fraîche.

- 8 crisp, sweet apples such as Gala apples
- 4 tablespoons lemon sugar (see Note)
- 4 tablespoons brown sugar
- 1 teaspoon cinnamon
- 8 large pieces lemon peel
- 3 tablespoons unsalted butter, softened
- 1 tablespoon dried cherries
- 1 vanilla bean
- 4 cinnamon sticks

Preheat the oven to 375° F.

Slice the bottoms off the apples and core them. Generously butter a large glass or porcelain dish and sprinkle with 2 tablespoons of the lemon sugar. Arrange the apples upright in the dish.

Fill the center of each apple with 1 teaspoon brown sugar, ⅛ teaspoon cinnamon, and 1 piece of lemon peel. Rub the top of each apple with ¼ tablespoon soft butter and sprinkle with more lemon sugar. Sprinkle the dried cherries around the apples and add the vanilla bean and cinnamon sticks to the dish. Bake the apples for 30 to 45 minutes until soft.

Note: I like making flavored sugars by layering sugar in a covered quart jar with an aromatic ingredient like fragrant rose petals, lemon peel, vanilla beans, or scented geranium leaves. Replenish the sugar as you use it, and replace the aromatic ingredients when their scent fades.

above: Lightly flavored with lemon zest and cinnamon, these baked apples are extremely easy to make and are well worth any effort.
opposite: Once cut, the devil's food cake was crumbly but moist, dark, and rich. Plain white plates were great for sampling. This crystal-handled fork is one of a kind—I'd love to have a whole set.

Chocolate DEVIL'S FOOD CAKE

Serves 8 to 10

This delicious recipe will make a three-layer devil's food cake, although I used two decorative fluted cake pans for my dessert buffet.

- 3 ounces unsweetened chocolate
- 1 teaspoon baking soda
- ½ cup boiling water
- 1 cup (2 sticks) unsalted butter, at room temperature
- 2 cups sugar
- 5 large eggs
- 3 cups unbleached all-purpose flour, sifted
- ¾ cup buttermilk
- 1 teaspoon vanilla extract Seven-Minute Frosting (recipe follows)

Preheat the oven to 350° F. Butter three 9-inch round cake pans or 2 decorative 9-inch round fluted pans.

Melt the chocolate in a double boiler over simmering water. In a bowl stir the baking soda into the ½ cup boiling water; stir this liquid into the chocolate. Set aside to cool slightly.

Using an electric mixer, cream the butter and sugar until the mixture is pale yellow in color. Add the eggs, one at a time, and continue to mix until thoroughly incorporated. Alternately add the flour and buttermilk in small amounts, and blend well.

Add the melted chocolate and the vanilla to the batter and stir well. Pour the batter into the prepared pans and bake for 30 minutes or until a cake tester comes out clean when inserted into the center of each cake. Remove the cakes from the oven and allow them to cool briefly in the pans before inverting onto racks. Allow the cakes to cool thoroughly, then frost them.

Seven-Minute Frosting

- 1½ cups sugar
- 2 large egg whites
- ½ cup water
- ⅛ teaspoon salt
- 1 tablespoon light corn syrup
- 1 teaspoon vanilla extract

In the top of a double boiler, combine the sugar, egg whites, water, salt, corn syrup, and vanilla. Place over simmering water and beat with a whisk or electric mixer for exactly 7 minutes. Remove from the heat and continue beating until the frosting is cool, thick, and fluffy, about 20 to 25 minutes. Use immediately, as the frosting will harden as it cools.

left: *This tin and copper mold was found at a tag sale. It made a lovely persimmon pudding that was tender and fragrant.*

below: *Blood oranges are available only during certain months. Squeeze extras and freeze the juice for sorbets and glazes such as this one.*

right: *The yellow pound cake is infused with citrus flavor by the addition of a hot lemon syrup while the cake is still hot. The decorations are slices of candied kumquats.*

above: *I bought this covered steamer mold many years ago because it was both heavy and sturdy and looked like it would last a very long time.* **right:** *Reversed onto a glass pedestal, the steamed ginger pudding was aromatic and appealing.*

Yellow Pound CAKE *with* BLOOD ORANGE GLAZE

Serves 10 to 12

Blood oranges have ruby red flesh and are wonderfully sweet and juicy; they make a delicious glaze. As a variation, this cake can be glazed with Lemon Syrup (recipe follows) and then decorated with candied kumquat slices.

Cake

- 1 cup (2 sticks) unsalted butter, at room temperature
- 3 cups sugar
- 1 teaspoon vanilla extract
- 6 large eggs
- 3 cups unbleached all-purpose flour, sifted twice, then measured
- 1 cup sour cream
- 2 teaspoons fresh lemon juice

Glaze

- 1 cup fresh blood orange juice
- ⅓ cup sugar
- 3 blood oranges, peeled and cut into segments

Preheat the oven to 350° F. Butter and flour a 10-inch turban-shaped cake mold.

To make the cake, in the bowl of an electric mixer cream together the butter, sugar, and vanilla. Beat in the eggs, one at a time, until thoroughly incorporated. Alternately add the flour and sour cream in small amounts, and blend well; add the lemon juice with the last addition. Pour the batter into the prepared cake pan and bake for 1 hour, or until the cake is lightly golden and a toothpick inserted in the center comes out clean. Cool the cake in the pan for 10 minutes, then turn out onto a rack to cool completely.

Meanwhile, prepare the glaze. In a saucepan, combine the blood orange juice and sugar. Cook over medium heat for 10 to 15 minutes to reduce the liquid to ⅓ cup. Cool slightly.

Transfer the cake to a cake stand or plate. Use a pastry brush to apply glaze to the top and sides of the cake. Arrange the orange segments around the base of the cake.

Lemon Syrup with Candied Kumquats

- ½ cup fresh lemon juice
- ½ cup sugar
- 3 kumquats, sliced crosswise

In a medium saucepan, combine the lemon juice and sugar. Cook over medium heat, for 10 minutes, to reduce the liquid to ½ cup.

Add the sliced kumquats to the syrup and cook the mixture over medium heat for 10 minutes. Remove the kumquats with a slotted spoon and arrange them on top or around the base of the cooled yellow pound cake. Use a pastry brush to apply the syrup as a glaze to the top and sides of the pound cake.

Steamed PERSIMMON PUDDING *with* PERSIMMON PURÉE

Serves 8

I used a melon-shaped mold for this exquisitely flavored pudding.

- 2 cups unbleached all-purpose flour
- 1 teaspoon baking soda
- ½ teaspoon baking powder
- ½ teaspoon salt
- ½ teaspoon ground cinnamon
- 2 teaspoons ground allspice
- ¼ teaspoon ground cloves
- 7 large, very ripe persimmons
- 4 large eggs, lightly beaten
- 1 cup heavy cream
- ¾ cup sugar
- 2 teaspoons vanilla extract
- ½ cup (1 stick) unsalted butter, melted

Butter a 1-quart covered steamed pudding mold and sprinkle with sugar. Shake out any excess sugar.

Sift together the flour, baking soda, baking powder, salt, cinnamon, allspice, and cloves.

Peel 3 of the persimmons, remove seeds, place the fruit in the bowl of a food processor, and purée. While puréeing, add the following ingredients one at a time through the feed tube: eggs, heavy cream, sugar, vanilla, and melted butter. Stir this mixture into the flour until well combined.

Pour the batter into the prepared pudding mold and place the lid on securely. Place the mold on a rack in a large stockpot filled with enough water to come halfway up the sides of the mold. Simmer, covered, over low heat for 50 minutes. Remove the lid; if the center of the pudding looks loose and too moist, or does not spring back when lightly pressed with your finger, recover the mold and continue to steam. Remove the mold from the pot and allow to cool for 5 to 10 minutes.

To unmold the pudding, run a knife around the edges while it is still warm. Carefully invert it onto a plate and lift off the mold. If it sticks, gently tap the mold with a wooden spoon.

Peel and seed the remaining 4 persimmons. Place them in the food processor and purée until smooth. Spoon the purée around the pudding and serve.

Dessert *Buffet*

Steamed Ginger PUDDING

Serves 6 to 8

Make sure you chop the crystallized ginger finely to give this pudding its subtle, rich flavor.

2¾ cups unbleached all-purpose flour
2 teaspoons baking powder
2 teaspoons ground ginger
1 teaspoon baking soda
½ teaspoon salt
2 teaspoons ground cinnamon
½ teaspoon ground allspice
¼ teaspoon ground cloves
¼ teaspoon grated nutmeg
2 large eggs, lightly beaten
1 cup milk
1 cup dark molasses
3 tablespoons unsalted butter, melted
½ cup finely chopped crystallized ginger

Butter a 2-quart covered steamed pudding mold and sprinkle with sugar. Shake out any excess sugar.

Sift together the flour, baking powder, ginger, baking soda, salt, cinnamon, allspice, cloves, and nutmeg.

In a separate bowl, whisk together the eggs, milk, molasses, and butter. Stir in the ginger. Add this to the sifted flour and stir until well combined.

Pour the batter into the prepared mold and place the lid on securely. Place the mold on a rack in a large stockpot filled with enough water to come halfway up the sides of the mold. Simmer, covered, over low heat for 1½ hours. Remove the mold from the pot and allow to cool for 5 to 10 minutes. To unmold the pudding, run a knife around the edges while it is still warm. Invert onto a serving plate and lift off the mold. If it sticks, gently tap the mold with a wooden spoon.

Steamed Brioche PUDDING

Serves 10 to 12

This pudding can be made in a glass baking dish or a metal cake pan. I used a turban-shaped cake mold to make it decorative and unique.

¾ cup sugar, plus more for sprinkling
1 cup golden raisins
  Zest and juice of 1 orange
  Zest of 2 lemons
1½ large loaves brioche (white bread can be substituted), crusts intact
1½ cups milk
1 cup heavy cream
6 large eggs
4 tablespoons dark rum
½ cup shelled unsalted pistachios
  Sour Lemon Cream Sauce (recipe follows)

Butter a 3-quart turban mold and sprinkle with sugar. Shake out any excess sugar.

In a small bowl, combine the raisins, orange juice and zest, and lemon zest; set aside for about 15 minutes to plump the raisins.

Cut the brioche into 2-inch chunks and put them into the prepared mold. Do not remove crusts.

In a mixing bowl, whisk together the milk, cream, eggs, ¾ cup sugar, and rum. Stir in the pistachios and the raisin–orange juice mixture. Pour over the bread cubes and stir lightly to distribute pistachios and raisins. Place a piece of wet parchment paper over the top of the mold and secure with a large rubber band. Place the mold on a large sheet of aluminum foil; bring the sides up to enclose the mold completely.

Place the mold on a rack in a large stockpot. Fill with enough hot water to come halfway up the sides of the

mold. Simmer, covered, over low heat for 2 hours. Remove the mold from the pot and allow to cool 5 to 10 minutes. To unmold, run a knife around the edges while it is still warm. Carefully invert the pudding onto a serving plate.

Serve with Sour Lemon Cream Sauce or softly whipped cream.

Sour Lemon Cream Sauce

Makes 2½ cups

2 cups heavy cream
½ cup sugar
  Grated zest of 1 lemon
6 large egg yolks
3 tablespoons fresh lemon juice

Combine the cream, sugar, and lemon zest in a medium saucepan and cook over medium-high heat until the mixture almost comes to a boil. Remove from the heat and set aside for 30 minutes to steep.

In a medium bowl, whisk the egg yolks. Heat the cream mixture again to just below boiling. Pour a small amount of the scalded cream mixture into the yolks, whisking constantly. Then add the yolk mixture to the saucepan with the cream. Stir over medium-high heat until the mixture is thick enough to coat the back of a spoon, no more than 5 minutes; make sure the mixture does not come to a boil. Strain the sauce through a fine sieve into a clean bowl. Cover and chill in the refrigerator.

When cold, stir in the lemon juice. The lemon cream can be kept for up to 2 days, stored tightly covered in the refrigerator.

left and above: *This antique copper turban mold made an exquisite, shapely steamed brioche pudding.* **right:** *When steaming a pudding in a mold without a cover, first secure a piece of wet parchment paper over the top with a rubber band, drawing it tight over the mold. Set the mold on top of a large piece of foil, creating an envelope around it so water will not seep under the parchment.*

BUCHE
de Noël

Serves 20

This chocolate "yule log" is a traditional French Christmas dessert. For the cake, I used a 24 by 16-inch proofer tray, which is a commercial double-size sheet pan. You can also use two 13 by 11-inch jellyroll cake pans; use one for the "log" and one for the "branches."

Cake

- 1¼ cups plus 2 tablespoons sifted cake flour, non-self-rising
- 2 cups plus 1 tablespoon sugar
- 1 cup sifted unsweetened cocoa powder
- 1 tablespoon baking powder
- 1½ teaspoons salt
- 6 large eggs
- 1 cup plus 2 tablespoons vegetable oil
- 2 tablespoons vanilla extract
- 10 large egg whites

Espresso Cream Filling

- 1 cup heavy cream, scalded
- 5 ounces bittersweet Callebaut chocolate, finely chopped
- 3 tablespoons strong espresso, cooled
- 3 cups heavy cream, cold
- ¾ cup confectioners' sugar

Swiss Meringue Buttercream Icing

- 1 cup egg whites (6–8 egg whites)
- 2 cups sugar
- 2½ cups (5 sticks) unsalted butter, softened, cut into pieces
- ½ pound white chocolate, melted

Meringue Mushrooms (recipe follows)
Cocoa powder for dusting
Sprigs of evergreen

Preheat the oven to 350° F.

To make the cake, butter a 24 by 16-inch proofer tray (or two 13 by 11-inch jellyroll pans), then line it with parchment paper, leaving a 2-inch overhang on the short ends. Butter the parchment paper and the sides of the pan. Lightly dust the pan with flour and tap out the excess.

In a medium bowl, sift together the flour, 1½ cups of the sugar, the cocoa, baking powder, and salt.

In a large bowl, whisk the whole eggs, oil, and vanilla until frothy. Stir in the flour mixture until blended and thick.

In the bowl of an electric mixer, beat the egg whites until frothy. Increase the speed to medium-high and beat until soft peaks start to form. One teaspoon at a time, add the remaining sugar and continue beating the whites until stiff but not dry.

Fold one-third of the beaten egg whites into the egg and flour mixture. One third at a time, gently fold in the remaining whites. Do not overmix. Scrape the batter into the prepared pan and spread evenly.

Bake the cake for 12 to 15 minutes, until it springs back when gently touched in the center. Run the tip of a knife around the edges of the pan. Cover the cake with a large piece of plastic wrap, and then cover the plastic with a damp linen towel. Invert the cake onto a baking rack. When it is just cool enough to handle, start at a long side and roll the cake, with the parchment paper and the towel, into a cylinder. Cool the rolled cake to room temperature.

To make the filling, pour the scalded heavy cream over the chopped chocolate and allow it to sit for 1 or 2 minutes until the chocolate melts. Stir until smooth. Add 1 tablespoon of the espresso and continue to blend until the espresso is incorporated. Set aside in a bowl to cool.

In the bowl of an electric mixer, whip the cold heavy cream and confectioners' sugar until thick. Add the remaining espresso and continue beating at high speed. Gradually add the chocolate mixture and beat until light and fluffy. Set aside.

To make the icing, combine the egg whites and sugar in a large mixing bowl and place over simmering water (the bowl should not touch the water), whisking occasionally until the mixture is warm and the sugar has dissolved. Remove from the heat.

Using an electric mixer, beat the mixtue on high speed until stiff peaks form. Continue beating on medium speed until the meringue reaches room temperature. Still on medium speed, add the butter, one piece at a time, until the butter is well blended. Scrape down the sides and bottom of the bowl from time to time.

Beat the buttercream at high speed for a minute or two. Add the melted white chocolate and continue beating at high speed until evenly blended, again scraping down the sides of the bowl from time to time. Refrigerate until ready to use.

Unroll the cooled cake slowly, carefully removing the parchment paper, plastic wrap, and towel. Evenly spread the cake with the Espresso Cream Filling. Starting from the other end, reroll the filled cake into a "log."

Chill the cake for at least 1 hour before proceeding.

Cut off each end of the roll on the angle, and use these pieces as "limbs." Ice the cake log with the buttercream icing, using a small metal spatula.

Decorate the log with Meringue Mushrooms and dust with cocoa powder. Garnish the serving platter with sprigs of evergreens.

Meringue Mushrooms

Makes about 40 mushrooms

6   egg whites
     Pinch salt
¼   teaspoon cream of tartar
1   teaspoon vanilla extract
1½ cups superfine sugar
     Cocoa powder for dusting
6   ounces semisweet chocolate, melted

Preheat the oven to 225° F., line 2 large baking sheets with aluminum foil.

In a large bowl, beat the egg whites until foamy. Add the salt, cream of tartar, and vanilla and continue beating. Add the sugar 1 teaspoon at a time, beating for about 30 seconds between each addition. When all the sugar has been added, beat for an additional 6 minutes. The egg whites should be very stiff, glossy, and extremely smooth, but not dry.

To make the mushrooms, spoon the mixture into 2 pastry bags, fitted with a ½-inch round tip for the stems and a ⅝-inch tip for the caps. Holding the ⅝-inch tip close to a baking sheet, press out round tops for the mushroom caps. (Any unwanted points can be smoothed with a finger dipped in cold water.)

For the stems, use the smaller tip. Hold the pastry bag in one hand and a small sharp knife in the other. Press out the stem, allowing ¾ to 1 inch in height, and then cut off the meringue with the knife. The stem will have a

flat end that will adhere more easily to the cap. Lightly dust the stems with cocoa powder.

Reduce the oven temperature to 200° F. and bake the meringues for 1½ to 2 hours, until they are dry to the touch and can be lifted from the foil. Cool completely.

To assemble, with a small spatula spread a thin layer of melted choco-

late on the underside of the cap. Dip the flat tip of the stem into the chocolate and affix to the cap. Turn upside down and dry. (Egg cartons turned upside down are excellent racks for this purpose.)

above: *Once decorated, the Bûche de Noël is certain to be the centerpiece of any holiday dessert buffet.*

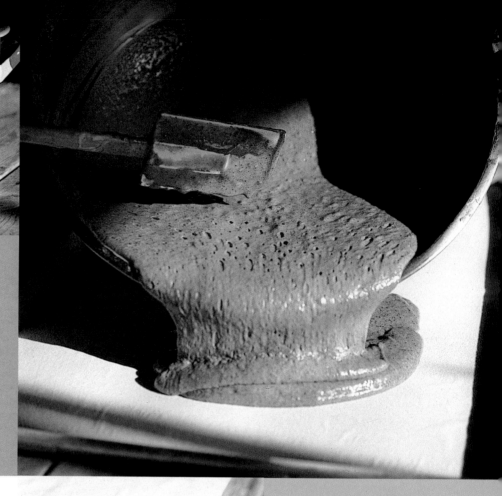

*As a serious baker and dessert maker,
I love the simplicity of all the ingredients used in the baker's craft: excellent
unbleached flours, the freshest eggs (I
raise my own laying hens), and various
sugars stored in wide-mouthed jars for
easy dipping and measuring.*

first: The chocolate Bûche de Noël is a
bit time consuming to assemble, but fairly
easy to make. Bake a large sheet of the
cake to yield a long log. The sheet pan is
first buttered, then lined with parchment
paper before the batter is poured in evenly.

second: It is imperative to roll the
cake while it is still warm. Right after the
cake has finished baking, cover it with a
large piece of plastic wrap and cover the
plastic with a damp linen towel. When it is
cool enough to handle, start from one long
end and carefully roll up the cake, using
the parchment paper, plastic wrap, and
towel as part of the process.

third: Allow the cake to cool to room temperature. Then carefully unroll the cooled cake, discarding the plastic, towel, and parchment. Spread the espresso cream filling evenly on the cake. Reroll the cake, starting from the other long end.

fourth: Chill the cake for at least one hour before decorating. Place it seam side down on a parchment paper–covered work surface. I cut off the ends of the 24 by 16-inch log on angles and use the trimmings as "tree limbs" for the log. If using two jelly roll pans, cut one log on the diagonal to create "limbs."

fifth: The log now has "sawn-off branches." Except for the ends of the branches, the entire log is iced thickly with the meringue buttercream. Use a spatula to apply the icing, shaping the icing to simulate a snow-covered tree trunk.

sixth: The cake is transferred to a serving tray and decorated with appropriately placed meringue mushrooms. These can be made in a variety of sizes.

seventh: For final display, real sprigs of evergreens can be arranged decoratively and the whole log can be dusted with a sprinkling of cocoa powder.

18

A **Birthday** DINNER *of Gifts*

Serves 40

✴ *Duck*-Filled Beggar's Purses

Mushroom-Filled Beggar's Purses

Christmas *Pasta* "Crackers" with Chèvre, Brown Butter, and *Mint Pesto*

Stuffed Fillets of *Beef* with *Leek* Ribbons

Caramelized *Shallots* and Snow *Peas* ✴

Golden-Candied Poached *Pears*

A Birthday DINNER *of Gifts*

MY FRIEND CARMEN ROBINSON AND I RECENTLY CONSPIRED TO CELEBRATE OUR
DEAR FRIEND SUSAN CHESNOFF'S FIFTIETH BIRTHDAY. FOR THIS MOMENTOUS
OCCASION, WE DEVISED A SURPRISE SIT-DOWN DINNER FOR FORTY, TO BE GIVEN AT
MY HOME THE SUNDAY EVENING BEFORE CHRISTMAS. I PLANNED A MENU THAT
REFLECTED THE HOLIDAY SPIRIT AND THE BIRTHDAY FESTIVITIES. ALL THE FOOD
WAS A WRAPPED "GIFT" OF SOME SORT: CREPE AND PHYLLO POUCHES, PASTA
"CRACKERS," FILLETS OF BEEF TIED WITH LEEK RIBBONS, AND GLISTENING PEARS
DECORATED WITH CARAMEL BOWS. THE EVENING WAS BEAUTIFUL. SUSAN WAS
SURPRISED, SHOCKED REALLY, WHEN SHE AND HER HUSBAND, RICHARD, CAME TO
PICK ME UP FOR DINNER AT EIGHT. I TOOK THEM TO SEE THE DECORATIONS I HAD
CREATED IN MY BARN. THERE, THE GUESTS HAD ALL GATHERED, DAZZLING IN
BLACK TIE. COCKTAILS AND CHAMPAGNE WERE SERVED FOR ABOUT AN HOUR IN THE
BARN. AT NINE, WE BEGAN OUR PROMENADE TO THE MAIN HOUSE THROUGH THE
DARK BUT STARRY NIGHT. BECAUSE MY HOME IS NOT VERY LARGE, I TURNED EACH
OF THE FOUR FIRST-FLOOR ROOMS INTO A DINING ROOM. A DIFFERENT COLOR
SCHEME PREVAILED IN EACH ROOM, BUT THE COMMON THREAD WAS THE HOLIDAY
SEASON, WITH SILVER AND GOLD AND CHRISTMAS TREES AND ORNAMENTS APLENTY.

previous page: *The library table was set with white and black and silver lustre; my Irish damask napkins were monogrammed with big black M's.*
below: *In the green sitting room a mercury glass butler's ball was illuminated by a chandelier tied with turquoise silk ribbons.*

above: *For the porch table, six dozen pale pink parrot tulips were massed in a compote. We chose pale yellow glassware to enhance this bouquet.* **below:** *I placed wide black silk bows on the table and silver-leaf cookie stars on the tree in the library.*

below: *Susan's menu was designed by her husband, Richard. He used a charming photograph of Susan taken when she was a child and had it printed in its original pale tints on the front of a folded card. The menu was printed inside.*

above and below: *Making the crepe beggar's purses. The crepes were cut with a biscuit cutter. A tablespoon of the filling was centered on the crepe and then the edges were turned up and tied with a poached chive. The crepe and phyllo pouches were the first "gifts" we offered the guests at Susan's party. I used many of my silver trays for this holiday party, and festively arrayed them with silk ribbons and Christmas balls.*

Duck-Filled
BEGGAR'S PURSES

Makes 80

These savory pouches are made very small so that they are bite-sized; that way, the flaky phyllo pastry does not crumble everywhere.

    4 whole duck breasts
    ½ cup dried cranberries, chopped
    ½ cup dark raisins, chopped
    3 sprigs fresh rosemary, chopped
       Salt and freshly ground pepper
    2 bunches chives
    2 1-pound boxes frozen prepared
       phyllo dough, thawed
    1 cup (2 sticks) unsalted
       butter, melted

Preheat the oven to 400° F.

Using a sharp knife, score the fatty skin on the duck breasts in a cross-hatching pattern and arrange on a roasting pan, fat side up. Roast the breasts 30 minutes. When cool enough to handle, discard the skin, bones, and fat, and chop the meat finely.

In a large bowl, combine the duck, cranberries, raisins, rosemary, salt, and pepper until well mixed.

Blanch the chives for 3 minutes in boiling water, then immediately drain and plunge into ice water. Drain again, then spread the chives flat on a dish towel.

To assemble, spread 1 sheet of phyllo dough on a clean surface, keeping the rest of the dough covered with a damp dish towel. Brush the entire surface with butter, then top with another sheet of phyllo. Repeat twice for a total of 4 sheets of phyllo dough one on top of another, brushing butter between each layer. Using a sharp knife, cut the layered dough into 6 squares. Place a heaping tablespoon of duck filling in the center of each phyllo square. Pull the corners up to the center and gather

the dough, pinching it closed over the filling. Tie each bundle securely with a single chive. Using sharp scissors, snip the dough off one inch above the chive ribbon so that the tops are even. The purses can be frozen on parchment-lined sheets, well wrapped, at this point. To serve, preheat the oven to 350° F. Place the purses on baking sheets and bake for 10 to 15 minutes, until golden brown. Serve hot.

Mushroom-Filled
BEGGAR'S PURSES

Makes 40

Beggar's purses tied with lengths of chive are a delicate way to serve tiny crepes filled with a fine mushroom mixture. Use shiitake, porcini, portobello, or chanterelle mushrooms.

Crepe Batter

    1 cup unbleached all-purpose
       flour, sifted
    1 pinch salt
    2 cups milk
    2 large egg yolks
    4 large eggs
    ½ cup clarified unsalted butter
       (see Note)

Mushroom Filling

    3 pounds wild mushrooms,
       cleaned and finely diced
    4 tablespoons (½ stick) unsalted
       butter
       Salt and freshly ground pepper
    ½ cup white wine
    ¼ cup finely chopped fresh parsley
    ⅛ cup finely chopped chervil
    1 bunch chives

To make the crepes, in a blender mix together the flour, salt, and milk. Add the egg yolks and eggs, blending until well combined. Add 4 tablespoons of the clarified butter. Allow the batter to rest for at least 30 minutes.

Heat a crepe pan over medium heat until hot. Remove the pan from the heat and, using a paper towel, wipe it with a teaspoon of the remaining clarified butter. Add 2 tablespoons of batter and tilt and swirl the pan until the batter coats the bottom; add more if necessary.

Return to the heat and cook until little bubbles form on the surface of the crepe, about 45 seconds. Flip and cook the second side briefly, about 25 seconds. Do not brown.

Repeat with the remaining batter, buttering the pan with additional clarified butter as needed.

Stack the crepes and keep them covered in plastic wrap until ready to use. These can be made several hours before the final assembly.

To make the filling, wrap the mushrooms a few at a time in a kitchen towel and squeeze to press out as much moisture as possible.

In a large pan, melt the butter over medium heat. Add the mushrooms, salt, and pepper and sauté until browned, about 7 to 10 minutes. Add the wine and continue to cook until the liquid has evaporated, 3 or 4 minutes. Remove from the heat and stir in the fresh parsley and chervil.

To assemble the purses, preheat the oven to 200° F. Blanch the chives for 3 minutes in boiling water, then immediately drain and plunge into ice water. Drain again, then spread the chives flat on a dish towel.

Using a 6-inch round cutter with a fluted edge, cut rounds from each crepe. Place 1 tablespoon of the mushroom filling in the center of each round. Gather up the edges over the center and tie securely with a single chive. Place the purses on baking

sheets or in microwave-proof baking dishes that are lined with parchment paper.

Heat the filled beggar's purses in the oven for 5 or 6 minutes or in the microwave on medium for 1 to 2 minutes. Serve hot.

Note: To clarify butter, melt it in a small saucepan over low heat. Remove from heat and allow the milk solids to settle to the bottom. Skim any foam from the surface, then carefully pour off the clarified butter, leaving the solids behind. One and a half sticks of butter will yield the half cup clarified butter required for the crepes.

above: *An antique drawnwork cloth covered the parlor table. It was one of a pair I found in a Greenwich shop, yellowed and dingy but otherwise in very good shape. After a careful laundering and a pinned tabletop drying, the cloths were perfect for a formal dinner. The place setting was a mix of Wedgwood, Spode, Depression glass, and silver and pearl flatware. A mirrored tray in the center of the table held beribboned candlesticks and shiny Christmas balls.*

Christmas PASTA "CRACKERS" with CHEVRE, Brown BUTTER, and Mint PESTO

Makes 40

In England the Christmas table traditionally includes a decorative gift called a cracker. Little presents are stuffed inside cardboard rolls, which are then wrapped and tied. A gunpowder cap is inserted, and before opening, each recipient pops his gift. I made my "crackers" from striped pasta, filled with a spinach-cheese combination. I did not include any "poppers"!

2 cups golden raisins
3 tablespoons extra-virgin olive oil
2 cups (4 sticks) plus 2 tablespoons unsalted butter
8 shallots, peeled and chopped
5 pounds fresh spinach, washed, drained, and stemmed
1½ cups pine nuts, lightly toasted (see Note)
14 ounces soft chèvre, crumbled
2 teaspoons freshly grated nutmeg
Salt and freshly ground pepper
4 to 5 bunches chives
8 pounds prepared pasta in sheets, 13 by 18 inches each (see Note)
1 large egg, lightly beaten
Mint Pesto (recipe follows)

To make the filling, plump the raisins in a bowl of hot water for 15 minutes.

Preheat the oven to 300° F. In a large skillet, heat 2 tablespoons of the olive oil and 2 tablespoons of the butter over medium-high heat. Add the shallots and sauté until tender, about 8 to 10 minutes. Add the spinach and stir until wilted, about 5 minutes. Allow to cool completely, then chop the mixture coarsely. Transfer to a large mixing bowl.

Drain the raisins and add them with the pine nuts to the spinach and shallots, tossing together well. Stir in the chèvre and season with nutmeg, salt, and pepper.

To assemble the crackers, blanch the chives for 3 minutes in boiling water. Drain, then immediately plunge the chives into a bowl of ice water. Drain again, then spread the chives flat on a dish towel.

Using pinking shears or a pastry wheel, cut the pasta sheets into 8-inch squares. While working, keep a damp dish towel over the pasta to keep it moist and pliable.

Working with one pasta square at a time and keeping the stripes vertical, use a small pastry brush to brush the top edge with the beaten egg. Next, apply a ½-inch strip of beaten egg 1 inch in from either side; this will enable you to form a waterproof seal when closing up your pasta cracker, and allow for a nice ruffle on the edge.

Place 3 to 4 tablespoons of filling in the center of the pasta square. Fold the bottom edge up over the filling, then fold the top edge down so that it overlaps no more than ½ inch. Gently smooth and press the seam to seal.

Next, pinch the cracker closed 1 inch in from each side and tie with blanched chives, allowing the edges to ruffle. Be careful not to allow the filling to seep out of the pasta. Transfer to a baking sheet lined with parchment paper and keep covered with a damp dish towel. Repeat, filling the remaining pasta squares.

Bring a large stockpot of water to a boil with the remaining tablespoon of olive oil. Place a few pasta crackers in at a time and cook for 20 minutes. Remove to a rack with a slotted spoon.

Keep warm in the oven while the rest of the crackers cook.

To make the brown butter, in a skillet melt the 2 cups of butter over medium-high heat. Continue to cook until the butter is a nutty brown. Keep warm until ready to serve.

Place one cracker on each serving plate and drizzle with the brown butter. Garnish with mint pesto.

Note: To toast the pine nuts, spread them evenly on a baking sheet and place in a preheated 350° F. oven for 5 minutes. Shake often to ensure even toasting. The nuts are toasted when you can first smell them; watch that they don't burn.

I ordered the red and green pasta from La Romagnola Gourmet Pasta, 2720 North Forsyth Road, Winter Park, Florida (800) 843-8359. For a less Christmasy meal, use sheets of regular fresh pasta.

Mint Pesto

Yields 3 cups

4 bunches fresh mint, washed and dried
4 teaspoons oregano leaves
4 tablespoons fresh lemon juice
2 cups extra-virgin olive oil
1 cup pine nuts
8 garlic cloves, peeled
Salt and freshly ground pepper

In a blender or food processor, combine the mint, oregano, lemon juice, olive oil, pine nuts, garlic, salt, and pepper and purée until smooth.

Store, refrigerated, in a covered container until you are ready to use it. If made more than 2 days in advance, freeze the pesto.

Pasta "crackers" made a delightful appetizer. A little brown butter is spooned over the pasta, and each cracker is served with small dollops of mint pesto. I ordered this striped pasta from a supplier in Florida who has the special machine required to make the stripes. The dough comes in sheets and can be used for ravioli, cannelloni, and more unusual pasta dishes such as our "gifts."

Birthday DINNER

Stuffed FILLETS *of* BEEF *with* LEEK RIBBONS

Serves 40

Filled with a savory vegetable mixture and elegantly tied with decorative leek ribbons, these fillets of beef are both festive and delectable.

- 4 tablespoons extra-virgin olive oil
- 16 carrots, peeled and julienned
- 16 red bell peppers, seeded and julienned
- 7 leeks, washed thoroughly and julienned
- ¼ cup fresh thyme leaves
  Salt and freshly ground pepper
- 6 whole beef fillets, trimmed of fat
  Cotton kitchen string
- 1½ cups (3 sticks) unsalted butter
  Poached Leek Ribbons (recipe follows)

Preheat the oven to 400° F.

In a large skillet, heat the olive oil and sauté the carrots, peppers, leeks, and thyme for 10 minutes or until just tender. Season with salt and pepper to taste. Allow to cool.

Slice each fillet lengthwise about ¾ inch deep, making sure not to slice through the meat entirely. Fill each slit with an equal portion of the vegetable mixture. Cut the kitchen string into 8-inch lengths. Firmly close up the fillets and secure by tying the string into knots spaced 2 inches apart. In a large skillet, brown each fillet in 4 tablespoons of butter over medium-high heat, cooking each side for 5 minutes. Remove and tie a poached leek ribbon into a knot between each length of kitchen string; secure the knots with wooden toothpicks. Roast the fillets at 400° in a large roasting pan for 10 minutes, then reduce the heat to 350° for an additional 25 to 30 minutes for medium-rare. Allow the fillets to rest for 5 minutes. Remove the kitchen string and slice the fillets in 2-inch-thick rounds to serve. Garnish with bows made from additional poached leek ribbons.

Poached Leek Ribbons

- 12 large leeks

Choose long untrimmed leeks. Wash them without cutting.

Fill a large flat pan halfway with water. Bring the water to a boil and reduce to a simmer. Place a few leeks at a time in the hot water and poach until the outer leaves are just tender and bright green, about 3 to 5 minutes. Immediately remove the outer leaves and immerse in a large bowl filled with ice water. Continue poaching until all the leaves are separated.

Remove the leaves from the ice water and dry on dish towels. Cover with plastic wrap. These can be made a day ahead and refrigerated, wrapped in plastic.

Caramelized SHALLOTS *and* SNOW PEAS

Serves 40

Sweet and slightly crunchy, the caramelized shallots and blanched snow peas are a nice, unexpected addition to the menu.

- ½ cup (1 stick) unsalted butter
- ⅓ cup sugar
- 4 pounds shallots, peeled
- 3 pounds snow peas, stems and strings removed

In a large skillet, melt the butter with the sugar over medium heat. Add the shallots, stir gently to coat them with the syrup, and cook until the syrup is browned and the shallots are tender, about 20 minutes.

Fill a large stockpot three-quarters full of water and bring to a boil over high heat. Add the snow peas in batches. Blanch them briefly until bright green, about 1 minute, then immediately remove them with a slotted spoon. Serve hot alongside the caramelized shallots.

opposite: *Tied with cotton string to enclose the stuffing, the fillets of beef are quickly browned. The meat is then tied with extra-long leek ribbons and roasted. Additional bows made from poached leek leaves are used to decorate the sliced fillet before it is served on the dinner plates.*

left: *The julienned vegetables are gently sautéed with thyme before they are stuffed into each fillet of beef. This filling can be varied with wild mushrooms, truffles, or grains, if one desires.*

Birthday DINNER

Golden-Candied
POACHED PEARS

Serves 40

Use the most perfect pears you can find for this very special dessert: overripe fruit will result in sogginess and the dessert might collapse. If underripe, the pears will not poach well.

- 40 ripe Comice or Bosc pears with stems
  - Juice of 2 lemons
- 8 cups (2 bottles) white wine
- 8 cups water
- 2 cups honey
- 2 vanilla beans
- 2 star anise
- 40 black peppercorns
  - Cheesecloth
  - Pear Pastry Cream (recipe follows)
- 40 Golden Sugar Bows (recipe follows)
  - Caramel Sauce (recipe follows)
  - Golden Sugar Glaze (recipe follows)

Peel the pears carefully, leaving the stems intact. Cut off a small amount of the bottom so that the pears can stand upright. As you peel the pears, immerse them in a large bowl of cold water with the lemon juice. This will keep them from discoloring until ready to poach.

Cook the pears in batches to avoid overcrowding. In a large stockpot bring the wine, water, honey, vanilla beans, star anise, and peppercorns to a boil. Reduce the liquid to a simmer and gently add a batch of the pears, placing cheesecloth over the pears to keep them submerged. Allow them to simmer for 20 to 30 minutes until they are just tender. Remove the pears from the stockpot to a baking sheet lined with parchment paper and allow them

to cool. Repeat with the remaining pears.

When the pears have cooled, cut them in half horizontally. Using a melon baller, scoop out the pulp from the bottom half, creating a small cavity. Discard the core and reserve the pulp to use in the pastry cream filling.

Make the Pear Pastry Cream and refrigerate until ready to assemble the dessert.

Make 40 Golden Sugar Bows.

Make the Caramel Sauce and keep warm until ready to use.

To assemble the dessert, fill the cavity of each pear with 1 to 2 tablespoons of the Pear Pastry Cream and gently press the two halves together.

Just before serving, make the Golden Sugar Glaze and drizzle evenly over each pear to coat. Place pears on individual serving plates.

Garnish each stem with a Golden Sugar Bow, and then pour a spoonful of the warm Caramel Sauce around each pear.

Pear Pastry Cream

- 2½ cups milk
- 1½ vanilla beans
- 8 large egg yolks
- ½ cup sugar
- 1 pinch salt
- 3 tablespoons cornstarch
- 1 teaspoon ground ginger
- 2 tablespoons unsalted butter
- 1 cup pulp of poached pears, finely chopped (see recipe above)
- 2 tablespoons brandy

In a medium saucepan, scald the milk with the vanilla beans. Remove the vanilla beans, split them in half lengthwise, and scrape the seeds into the milk for additional flavor.

Beat the egg yolks, sugar, salt, cornstarch, and ginger until pale yellow. Slowly add the hot milk in small increments, constantly beating the egg yolk mixture. Continue adding the milk in this fashion, then transfer the mixture to the top of a double boiler. Over low heat, add the butter and continue stirring, until the mixture coats the back of a spoon, about 10 to 15 minutes. Immediately remove the top half of the double boiler from the heat and place in a large pan filled with ice water, whisking briskly to cool.

Place the pulp from poached pears into a large saucepan and cook over medium heat for 15 minutes, allowing the liquid to evaporate. Stir this into the cooled pastry cream. Add the brandy. When the mixture has cooled to room temperature, cover with plastic wrap and refrigerate.

Golden Sugar
Glaze and
Sugar Bows

This recipe makes enough caramel to glaze 40 pears, or to make 42 sugar bows. Make the bows in two batches for easier handling.

- 4 cups sugar
- ½ cup water

To make the glaze, in a heavy saucepan, preferably one with a pouring lip, heat the sugar and the water over medium-high heat until the mixture forms a golden brown syrup, about 10 minutes. Do not stir. Dip the bottom of the pan into a bowl of ice water to stop the caramel from cooking.

To make the bows, prepare the glaze. On baking sheets lined with parchment paper, form bows by drizzling syrup from the pan, about 1 tablespoon of syrup for each. Allow the

bows to cool until hard and then peel
them off the parchment paper. The
syrup can be heated again to keep it
thin enough to pour. Never stir the
caramel syrup as this makes it bubble
and lose its clarity.

Caramel Sauce

6 cups sugar
1 cup water
3 pints heavy cream

In a saucepan, heat the sugar and
water over medium-high heat until the
mixture forms a golden brown syrup,
about 15 to 20 minutes. Do not stir at
this time.

Add the heavy cream all at once; stir
with a wooden spoon and reduce heat
to medium. Cook for a few minutes
until the mixture is of a uniform, thick
caramel consistency. Transfer the
syrup to a warm bowl and keep it
warm in a pan of hot water until you
are ready to use it.

*The poached pear dessert was a big
success. The pear itself is poached,
then hollowed out and filled with a
pear-flavored pastry cream. It is
glazed with a thin coating of caramel
and decorated with a caramelized
sugar bow. When choosing pears for
poaching, be careful to select unblemished ripe fruit with long stems. I melt
my sugar for caramel in an unlined
copper sugar pot. The liquid flows
evenly from this sort of pot, and the
pouring lip makes the work a lot easier.*

19

NEW TRADITIONS *for* **Christmas**

Serves 2 0

Potato Pancakes with Pink Applesauce or Osetra Caviar

Apple–*Butternut Squash* Soup ✴

Venison Bourguignon

Fresh *Black Pepper* Noodles ✴ *Cranberry* Chutney

✴ Braised *Brussels Sprouts*

Pear Tarts ✴ Warm Spiced Tea

NEW TRADITIONS *for* Christmas

ONCE MY HOUSE IS ALL DECORATED FOR THE HOLIDAY SEASON, I USUALLY TRY TO PLAN A FEW SPECIAL LUNCHES AND DINNERS TO TAKE ADVANTAGE OF THE FESTIVE AMBIENCE. I HAD THIS CHRISTMAS LUNCHEON, FOR EXAMPLE, FOR THE ADVERTISING DEPARTMENT OF MY MAGAZINE. I DID NOT WANT THE TABLES TO BE TOO FORMAL, SO I USED AS "CLOTHS" TWO REMNANTS OF INGRAIN CARPETS, PIECES THAT WERE CLEAN LEFTOVERS OF SOME RESTORED RUGS FOR MY HOUSE. THE COLORS WERE DEEP JEWEL TONES THAT LOOKED GOOD IN THE COUNTRY KITCHEN AND ON THE PORCH WHERE I PLANNED TO SEAT EVERYONE. I CHOSE THE GLASSWARE FOR ITS DEEP COLORS AS WELL—AMETHYST, TEAL, RUBY—AND USED DRABWARE DINNER PLATES, SALAD PLATES, AND FIRST-COURSE PLATES OF BROWN AND WHITE TRANSFER AND BLUE LUSTRE. THE MENU WAS A HOMEY COMBINATION THAT APPEALED TO ALL. IT WAS ESPECIALLY WELL RECEIVED, I THINK, BECAUSE IT WAS HEARTY WITHOUT BEING TOO HEAVY, AND BECAUSE IT CONTAINED INGREDIENTS THAT WERE NOT ENTIRELY FAMILIAR TO MOST OF THE GUESTS, LIKE OSETRA CAVIAR AND VENISON AND OLD-FASHIONED POTATO PANCAKES. WE STARTED THE MEAL WITH A BUTTERNUT SQUASH SOUP SWEETENED WITH APPLES, AND FINISHED WITH PEAR TARTS AND WARM SPICED TEA, BRINGING THE MEAL TO A WONDERFUL END.

previous page: *One group of guests was seated on the porch, where the dining table was set between two old-fashioned Christmas trees. I recently discovered at a tag sale napkins that are an elegant two-toned damask of cream and amethyst. The initials inspired imaginative identities made up for these "long-lost relatives." The gold and brown ingrain carpet makes a bold tablecloth, and the tree behind the table was covered with scores of old glass ornaments.* above: *The butternut squash soup was served in square Depression glass bowls. I set the table with Bakelite flatware mixed with old oversized French silver plate.*

POTATO PANCAKES
with *Pink Applesauce* or *Osetra Caviar*

Makes 40 to 45 pancakes

I don't know of anyone who doesn't love crispy potato pancakes. Topped with caviar or homemade applesauce, they're especially delicious.

12 Idaho potatoes, peeled
 8 large eggs, lightly beaten
   Salt and freshly ground pepper
2–3 cups extra-virgin olive oil
   Pink Applesauce (recipe follows)
 2 pints sour cream
 1 4-ounce tin osetra caviar

Grate the potatoes into long strips, using smooth strokes to run the potatoes across the grater. Immediately place the grated potato into a bowl of cold water.

Drain the potatoes and combine them in a large bowl with the eggs and salt and pepper to taste. Add enough of the olive oil to a large skillet to measure ¼ inch deep. Heat the oil over medium-high heat until hot but not smoking. Form the potato mixture into 40 to 45 pancakes, about 4 inches in diameter. Fry 5 or 6 at a time until golden brown on both sides, about 4 minutes in all. Change the oil as it turns brown. Drain the pancakes on paper towels. Keep the first batches warm in a low (150° F.) oven while preparing the rest.

Arrange 2 pancakes on each plate. Garnish one with a tablespoon of applesauce and sour cream, the other with a tablespoon of sour cream and a spoonful of caviar.

Pink Applesauce

Yields 3 cups

 2 lemons
 6 red Rome apples, cored and quartered
 1 cup no-sugar-added apple-cranberry juice

Juice the lemons and reserve the rinds.

Combine the apples, apple-cranberry juice, lemon juice, and rinds in a large saucepan. Cover and cook over low heat, stirring occasionally, for 35 to 40 minutes, until the apples are tender and the mixture thickens. Pass through a food mill. Refrigerate.

Apple–Butternut SQUASH SOUP

Serves 20

With no cream or flour, this vegetable-based soup is an excellent first course; it has little fat and few calories.

 2 quarts Vegetable Stock (recipe follows)
 6 butternut squash
 6 McIntosh apples
½ cup plus 2 tablespoons unsalted butter, melted
 1 cup chopped leek (white part only)
   Zest of ¼ orange
¼ teaspoon ground cinnamon
   Salt and freshly ground pepper
 4 leeks, trimmed, cleaned, and sliced

Prepare the vegetable stock. While it is reducing, prepare the soup.

Preheat the oven to 450° F.

Cut 4 butternut squash in half, and scoop out the seeds. Core and quarter the apples. Generously brush the butternut squash with ½ cup of the melted butter. Fill the center of each squash with the apples, place them in a roasting pan, cover with foil, and roast 35 to 40 minutes, or until tender when pricked with a fork. Scoop out the pulp from the skin, discarding the rind. Pass the squash pulp and apples through a food mill. Transfer to a large bowl, add 1 quart of the vegetable stock, and set aside.

Peel, seed, and cut into chunks the 2 remaining butternut squash. In a stockpot combine the squash, 1 tablespoon butter, chopped leek, orange zest, cinnamon, and 1 quart of the stock. Bring to a boil, then reduce the heat and simmer over medium-low heat for 35 to 40 minutes, until the squash is tender. Purée the mixture in a food processor until smooth.

In a large stockpot combine the two purées and season to taste with salt and pepper. Reheat or keep warm over low heat. Add a bit of hot water if the soup is too thick.

Place the remaining butter in a skillet. Add the sliced leeks and sauté over medium heat until softened, 5 to 6 minutes. Garnish each serving with some of the sautéed leeks.

Vegetable Stock

Makes 2 quarts

 5 large carrots, washed and cut into large pieces
 2 whole heads garlic, unpeeled
 4 medium onions, quartered
 4 parsnips, washed and cut in large pieces
 4 shallots, unpeeled
 6 leeks, washed and cut in large pieces
½ bunch thyme
½ bunch chervil
½ bunch parsley
 2 bay leaves
 3 ¼-inch pieces fresh ginger

2 McIntosh apples, cored and
   quartered
3 celery stalks, cut in large pieces
1 tablespoon whole peppercorns
6 quarts water

In a large stockpot, add the carrots,
garlic, onions, parsnips, shallots,
leeks, thyme, chervil, parsley, bay
leaves, ginger, apples, celery, and peppercorns. Pour the water over the vegetables and bring to a boil over
medium-high heat. Reduce the heat
and simmer for 2 hours.

Strain and discard the vegetables.
Continue cooking over medium heat
until reduced to 2 quarts, about
1 more hour.

above: *Two potato pancakes were
served on a pretty brown and white
dish, one topped with caviar and sour
cream, the other with pink applesauce and sour cream. If made small
enough, the pancakes can be eaten
with one's fingers, although these
were large enough to require a fork.*

clockwise from top left: *Ever since I was a child I have coveted old glass tree ornaments; unfortunately I am not a real collector at heart, otherwise I certainly would have amassed hundreds by now, instead of just enough to decorate two trees. Homemade pasta is highly flavored with freshly ground black pepper; the spiciness is excellent with the venison and the well-braised brussels sprouts. The festive holiday table was animated with great conversation. I really like this chutney made with fresh and dried cranberries, dried cherries, and fresh oranges; in fact, I like cranberries so much that I serve them in smooth and chunky sauces, relishes, pies, tarts, and chutneys as well as in cranberry cordial.*

Christmas

Venison BOURGUIGNON

Serves 20

I've always liked venison, but lately I eat less and less red meat unless it is in a dish as interesting as this stew.

1½ pounds carrots, peeled and cut in chunks
2 pounds Idaho potatoes, peeled and cut in chunks
1 pound bacon, sliced
1½ cups unbleached all-purpose flour
2 tablespoons sugar
½ teaspoon coarse salt
½ teaspoon freshly ground pepper
1 9-pound shoulder of venison, cut into 2-inch cubes
16 cups chicken stock, simmering
2 bottles dry red wine, such as Côtes-du-Rhône
4 bay leaves
2 bunches thyme, tied individually with kitchen string
10 garlic cloves, chopped
2 pounds red pearl onions, peeled
1 pound fresh shiitake mushrooms, stems removed, sliced, or fresh button mushrooms, sliced
3 McIntosh apples, peeled, cored, and cut into chunks
¼ cup chopped fresh parsley

Preheat the oven to 325° F.

Roast the carrots and potatoes in a large roasting pan for 2 hours, tossing them occasionally so they do not burn.

Cook half the bacon in a large heavy-bottomed casserole over medium heat until crispy. Remove and reserve the bacon, leaving the bacon fat in the casserole.

In a mixing bowl, combine the flour, sugar, and salt and pepper. Dredge the venison in the flour mixture until evenly coated on all sides. Pat off excess flour. Brown the venison in the skillet with the bacon fat over medium-high heat, working in batches so it is not overcrowded. Return all the browned meat to the casserole.

Add the stock, wine, bay leaves, thyme, and garlic to the meat. Cover the casserole and place in the oven for 30 minutes. Add the carrots and potatoes and cook 45 minutes longer.

Meanwhile, in a separate large skillet, brown the remaining bacon. Remove the bacon and leave the bacon fat. Combine the bacon with the previously cooked bacon and add it to the venison mixture in the casserole, then return it to the oven.

Braise the onions in the bacon fat over medium heat for 10 to 12 minutes, until brown. Remove the onions with a slotted spoon and drain on paper towels.

Brown the mushrooms in the bacon fat, adding a bit of olive oil if necessary. Remove with a slotted spoon and drain on paper towels.

Add the onions, mushrooms, and apples to the venison stew and cook 15 minutes, until the meat is tender and the sauce rich and thick. Remove the thyme and sprinkle the stew with parsley before serving.

Fresh BLACK PEPPER NOODLES

Serves 20

If you serve this meal buffet style, toss the noodles with a bit of extra-virgin olive oil to keep them from drying out. Use freshly ground coarse pepper, such as Tellicherry, Lampong, or Malabar.

7 cups unbleached all-purpose flour
12 large eggs
2 teaspoons coarse salt
2 teaspoons extra-virgin olive oil
2 tablespoons fresh, coarsely ground pepper
½ cup chopped fresh parsley

For convenience, prepare this recipe in 2 batches.

In a food processor, combine half of the flour, 5 of the eggs, and half of the salt, olive oil, and pepper. Lightly beat a sixth egg in a small bowl. Process the flour-egg mixture until a ball forms, adding the beaten egg in increments as necessary.

With a pastry scraper, cut the dough into pieces ½ inch wide by 2 inches long. Run each piece through the roller part of a pasta machine 4 times, starting with the widest position and closing the position by 2 notches with each roll. The last run should be through the linguine cutter. Hang the noodles to dry on a pasta rack or a clean clothing rack.

Repeat the steps with the remaining ingredients.

Just before serving, bring a large pot of salted water to a boil over high heat, add the noodles, and boil for 2 to 3 minutes. Drain and garnish with parsley.

Braised BRUSSELS SPROUTS

Serves 20

Slow cooking with butter ensures that the brussels sprouts are tender, not bitter.

8 pints brussels sprouts
4 tablespoons (½ stick) unsalted butter
Salt and freshly ground pepper

Preheat the oven to 450° F.

In a large pot, place the brussels sprouts in water to cover. Bring to a boil over medium-high heat and cook for 10 minutes. Drain well and toss them in a large roasting pan with the butter and salt and pepper to taste. Cover with parchment paper or foil and roast for 45 minutes, or until tender. Serve hot.

Christmas

Cranberry CHUTNEY

Serves 20

This chutney is my latest solution to how to prepare the ubiquitous and ever-popular cranberry for a holiday supper.

- 2 oranges
- 1 pound fresh cranberries, washed
- 6 ounces dried cranberries
- 8 ounces dried cherries
- 3 cinnamon sticks
- 4 garlic cloves, minced
- 2 tablespoons chopped fresh ginger
- ¼ cup packed brown sugar
- ¼ cup balsamic vinegar
- ½ cup apple cider

Zest the two oranges and squeeze their juice. Set aside a teaspoon of the zest for garnish.

In a large saucepan, combine the fresh cranberries, dried cranberries, dried cherries, orange juice and orange zest, cinnamon sticks, garlic, ginger, brown sugar, balsamic vinegar, and apple cider. Simmer the mixture over medium-low heat for 25 minutes, until the liquid is evaporated and the chutney is thick. Serve with the Venison Bourguignon, using the cinnamon sticks and reserved zest as garnish.

PEAR *Tarts*

Yields 20 tarts

Comice pears, either green or red, are excellent for this dessert; Anjou or Bartlett pears are also good, but they should be ripe and unblemished.

- 3½ cups sugar
- 4 pounds homemade puff pastry (see Note, page 160), or 4 1-pound boxes (8 sheets) frozen prepared puff pastry, thawed
- 10 ripe pears
- 2 teaspoons fresh lemon juice
- 2 large eggs, lightly beaten with 1 tablespoon cold water
- ½ cup (1 stick) unsalted butter, cut into small pieces

Line several baking sheets with parchment paper. Sprinkle ⅛ cup of the sugar on each puff pastry sheet and press lightly, using a rolling pin. Roll to less than ⅛ inch thick. With a 4½-inch fluted round cutter, cut out 20 individual tarts; reserve the excess pastry. Place the pastry circles, sugar side up, on the baking sheets and keep refrigerated until ready to bake.

Peel the pears and reserve them in a large bowl of cold water to cover mixed with the lemon juice. Remove them one at a time and cut in half lengthwise. Core and cut each half thinly almost to the stem, fanning out the slices. Place one pear half on each pastry circle, arranging the fans evenly.

With a sharp knife, cut out small pastry leaves using the excess pastry. Drape 2 leaves over each pear in a decorative manner. Brush all of each tart's pastry with the egg wash, dot each pear with butter, and sprinkle each tart with 1 tablespoon of the sugar.

Preheat the oven to 375° F. Bake the tarts for 10 to 15 minutes. Sprinkle each tart with an additional tablespoon of sugar and continue baking for an additional 10 minutes, or until the pastry is golden brown and the pears are caramelized by the sugar. Transfer the tarts to a baking rack to cool.

Warm Spiced TEA

Makes 20 cups

This tea is a wonderful addition to any winter meal.

- 6 oranges
- 4 lemons
- 2 cinnamon sticks
- 2 gallons water
- 16 tea bags
- 1½ cups honey

Zest and juice the oranges and the lemons. In a large pot, combine the zest and juices, cinnamon, water, and tea bags. Bring to a boil over medium-high heat, then remove and steep for 15 to 20 minutes. Strain the tea bags and return the pot to medium heat, adding the honey. Serve hot.

left: *Each year I try to make something to give to the young people in my family. I love Steiff toys, and so I bought many of their little teddies. As an appropriate home for these stuffed toys, I created oversized stockings.* **right:** *Gifts of homemade cookies were wrapped in individual cellophane bags. I used plaid and check taffeta ribbons to form bows.* **opposite:** *The delicious pear tart.*

20

Come for CHAMPAGNE and *Caviar*

Serves 30

Sugar Snap *Peas* with *Beet Horseradish* Dipping Sauce

Green Caviar on Red New *Potatoes* ✳ *Caviar* on Toast

Sevruga Caviar on *Sweet Potato* Rounds

✳ *Beet* Stars and Caviar

Quail Eggs with Caviar

Scandinavian *Shrimp* on Black Bread ✳ *Salmon* Rosettes with Mustard Sauce

Egg Salad Canapés

Come for CHAMPAGNE and *Caviar*

SUSAN MAGRINO HAS BEEN THE PUBLICIST FOR MY BOOKS FOR MORE THAN TEN YEARS. NOW WITH HER OWN AGENCY, SHE HAS A HECTIC LIFE AND A CRAZY LIFESTYLE: SHE LOVES PARTIES BUT RARELY FINDS TIME TO ENTERTAIN IN HER OWN HOME. I RECENTLY DECIDED TO TREAT HER TO A CATERED PARTY IN HER APARTMENT FOR HER BIRTHDAY. THE APARTMENT HAD BEEN DECORATED FOR THE CHRISTMAS HOLIDAYS BY MY DAUGHTER, ALEXIS (WHO IS ALSO SUSAN'S FRIEND), WITH A WHITE ARTIFICIAL TREE COVERED WITH OLD TINSEL AND ANTIQUE PINK AND GREEN BALLS, GIANT PINK AMARYLLIS IN MOSS-COVERED POTS, TINSEL GARLANDS, AND SILVER BALLS. ROUND MIRRORS FROM THE FIFTIES WERE ARRAYED ON ONE LIVING ROOM WALL AND REFLECTED ALL THE GLITTER, MAKING THE SPACE SEEM TWICE AS LARGE. SUSAN WANTED TO SERVE ONLY CHAMPAGNE AND MINERAL WATER ALONG WITH SIMPLE, UNUSUAL HORS D'OEUVRES. I TRIED TO MAKE THE FOOD COLORFUL, WHILE STILL IN KEEPING WITH THE FIFTIES-STYLE DECOR. WE DECIDED TO USE SUSAN'S COLLECTION OF FIRE KING GREEN DESSERT PLATES FOR THE FOOD. AN ODD GOLD MULTILAYERED STAND HAD BEEN IN MY ATTIC FOR A FEW YEARS; WITH ALEXIS'S PERMISSION, I SET IT ON THE COFFEE TABLE AND ARRANGED PLATES OF FOOD ON TOP; ALEXIS THEN HUNG SILVER BALLS ON IT!

previous page: *Susan served only Champagne in slender flutes at her party. A little Fire King refrigerator dish was the receptacle for the small pink-edged cocktail napkins that my mother made for her as a birthday present.* above: *In the living room of Susan's apartment, one long wall is hung with odd-sized round mirrors. They create a quite unusual reflection of the rest of the room, with its Heywood-Wakefield furniture and its examples of Susan's eclectic taste. We stacked Fire King plates for hors d'oeuvres and dessert, arranged food on large platters, and displayed the caviar in chalk basins full of crushed ice. These basins are the bottom halves of domed nineteenth-century ice boxes.*

Sugar Snap PEAS *with* Beet Horseradish DIPPING SAUCE

Serves 30

Beet horseradish, a mixture of grated beets and prepared white horseradish, is commonly available and gives this dipping sauce its delicate pink color.

2 pounds sugar snap peas, stem ends removed
2 tablespoons beet horseradish
1 teaspoon prepared horseradish
2 cups crème fraîche (page 40)
1 tablespoon finely chopped fresh dill
1 tablespoon chopped scallion
¼ teaspoon coarse salt

Bring a large pot of water to a boil. Add the sugar snap peas and blanch for 1 minute. Drain, then immediately plunge the peas into a bowl of ice water. Drain again and keep refrigerated until ready to serve.

In a medium bowl, mix the beet horseradish, plain horseradish, crème fraîche, dill, scallion, and salt. Arrange the sugar snap peas around a bowl of the dip on a serving plate.

Green CAVIAR *on* Red New POTATOES

Makes 30 hors d'oeuvres

The tasty green caviar, flavored with wasabi, a Japanese horseradish, adds a novel twist to this favorite canapé.

15 small red new potatoes, washed
1 cup crème fraîche (page 40)
2 ounces flying-fish caviar

In a heavy saucepan, cover the potatoes with cold water. Bring to a boil and cook until just tender, about 30 minutes. Drain and cool. Cut each potato in half. Place cut side down. With a melon baller, scoop out the top of each half to create a hollow.

In the bowl of an electric mixer, whip the crème fraîche until thick and fluffy. Fill the hollowed center of each potato half with a dollop of crème fraîche and top with caviar. Arrange on a serving tray.

CAVIAR *on* TOAST

Makes 40 hors d'oeuvres

Optional garnishes for this delectable hors d'oeuvre include hard-boiled egg yolks and egg whites pressed through a coarse strainer; finely chopped white onion; crème fraîche; capers; and lemon wedges.

10 thin slices firm white bread
7 ounces sevruga caviar

Preheat the oven to 350° F.

With a serrated bread knife, remove the crusts from the bread. Cut each slice into quarters, diagonally, to form 4 triangles. Arrange on a baking sheet.

Lightly bake the bread triangles for 5 to 10 minutes; flip over and continue toasting for 3 to 5 minutes. The bread should be dry and very lightly golden.

Arrange the tin of caviar in a bed of crushed ice, using a glass, pottery, or metal receptacle to hold the ice. Use a bone or silver spoon to serve the caviar. Arrange the bread triangles on a tray and allow guests to make their own canapés.

Sevruga CAVIAR *on* SWEET POTATO ROUNDS

Makes 30 to 35 hors d'oeuvres

Sevruga's rich taste balances nicely with the mellow flavor of sweet potatoes.

5 long, thin sweet potatoes, peeled
1 cup crème fraîche (page 40)
2 ounces sevruga caviar
Fresh chervil, parsley, or dill for garnish

In a large pot, boil the sweet potatoes until just soft, about 30 minutes. Allow them to cool, peel, then cut into ½-inch-thick slices.

Spoon a small dollop of crème fraîche onto each potato slice. Top with sevruga caviar. Garnish with a sprig of fresh herb and arrange on a platter.

BEET STARS *and* CAVIAR

Makes 35 hors d'oeuvres

You can also roast the beets (page 29) to prepare them. Use a cookie cutter that is small enough in diameter to fit within the beet slices.

10 medium beets, scrubbed
1 cup crème fraîche (page 40)
2 ounces flying-fish caviar

In a large pot of water boil the beets over medium-high heat for 30 to 40 minutes, or until tender when pierced. Allow the beets to cool slightly before slipping off the skins. Cut them into ¼-inch-thick slices, then, using a small star cookie cutter, cut each into a star. Store on trays lined with parchment paper.

In the bowl of an electric mixer, whip the crème fraîche until it is thick and fluffy. Spoon into a pastry bag fitted with a star tip, and pipe a dot of crème fraîche onto each beet star.

Spoon ½ teaspoon of green caviar over the crème fraîche and arrange the beet stars on a platter.

∗

Note on caviar: Most people shudder when they think of the expense of good fresh black caviar. This menu makes the most of not too much of a very good thing. For thirty guests, two 7-ounce tins of fresh sevruga caviar were sufficient. I also discovered an unusual and inexpensive caviar for this party to accompany the classic black of sevruga. This was Japanese flying-fish roe mixed with the hot Japanese green horseradish, wasabi. The result was a pungent and brilliant green caviar. I found it at my local gourmet market; it made quite a striking presentation, so do ask for it at Japanese markets or even restaurants. For this menu, plan on buying a 7-ounce tin of flying-fish roe, regardless of color, and a 4-ounce tin of large-egged red salmon roe.

There are essentially three sizes of black caviar: sevruga, with the smallest eggs, dark black, very tasty, and the least expensive; osetra, with medium eggs, golden gray in color, delicately flavored, and medium expensive; and beluga, with the largest eggs, gray or golden color, most delicately flavored, and the most expensive. Salmon, flying-fish, and whitefish roe are relatively inexpensive in comparison. In the holiday season, shop around for the best price and value, but expect to pay almost $200 for a 14-ounce tin of sevruga caviar.

above: *Everyone enjoyed the crispy blanched sugar snap peas. We served them spiraled around a Fire King bowl filled with a pink dipping sauce.* **left:** *The sevruga was the real luxury.* **below:** *Halves of red potatoes hold crème fraîche and green flying-fish caviar.*

We served sevruga caviar on boiled sweet potatoes topped with crème fraîche. If you whip crème fraîche, it gets nice and stiff and can be piped or mounded like whipped cream. But because of its non-sweet taste it works well with hors d'oeuvres, offering a variation from the usual sour cream.

Cooked beets were sliced and then cut into stars using cookie cutters. On the day of the party we discovered Japanese flying-fish caviar colored a bright green by the addition of wasabi. Crunchy and pungent, it was great atop the beets with a bit of crème fraîche.

clockwise from top left: *Tiny dilled shrimp on black bread squares were very popular; garnishes for each tray included silver tinsel and shiny holiday balls, all inedible, of course! We used quail eggs for the caviar toppings; the halved eggs were generously topped with red (salmon), black (sturgeon), and green (flying-fish) caviars and were served from large Fire King plates. The fanciful gold stand was put to good use displaying a variety of hors d'oeuvres. Pumpernickel bread rounds, very thinly sliced, were the base for salmon rosettes which used an excellent Homarus smoked salmon from a local market.*

QUAIL EGGS *with* CAVIAR

Makes 48
hors d'oeuvres

You can use regular chicken eggs here rather than quail eggs, but for a cocktail party, I think the smaller the eggs used, the better.

2 dozen quail eggs
3 ounces sevruga caviar
4 ounces salmon caviar
3 ounces flying-fish caviar
   Fresh dill for garnish

In a large saucepan, place one dozen eggs in enough water to cover. Bring the water to a boil. Immediately remove from the heat and allow the eggs to sit for 2 minutes. Using a slotted spoon, carefully remove the eggs and immerse them in a large bowl of cold water. Repeat this process for the remaining eggs, always starting with cold water.

Peel the eggs and cut them in half lengthwise. Spoon a small amount of caviar on the egg halves. Garnish with a sprig of fresh dill and arrange on a serving dish.

Scandinavian SHRIMP *on* BLACK BREAD

Makes 30
hors d'oeuvres

Pale pink and tender, these tiny shrimp can be found in gourmet stores at holiday time.

¾ cup mayonnaise, homemade if possible
1 tablespoon fresh lemon juice
1 teaspoon Dijon mustard
2 teaspoons prepared horseradish
1 scallion, finely chopped
1 celery stalk, finely chopped
¼ teaspoon dill seed
   Salt and freshly ground pepper
2 cups tiny Norwegian shrimp, cooked and well drained
1 loaf thinly sliced German black bread
   Fresh dill or chervil for garnish

In a large bowl, stir together the mayonnaise, lemon juice, Dijon mustard, horseradish, scallion, celery, dill seed, and salt and pepper to taste. Gently fold in the shrimp.

Trim the crusts off the bread slices and cut them into quarters. Spoon 1 teaspoon shrimp mixture on each square. Garnish with a sprig of dill or chervil and arrange on a platter.

SALMON ROSETTES *with* *Mustard Sauce*

Makes 30
hors d'oeuvres

Always try to use the finest freshly sliced smoked salmon, rather than the presliced packaged variety.

2 tablespoons Dijon mustard
1 tablespoon dry mustard
2 tablespoons sugar
1 tablespoon white wine
½ teaspoon coarse salt
½ teaspoon freshly ground pepper
1 tablespoon chopped fresh dill
1 teaspoon prepared horseradish
½ pound thinly sliced smoked salmon
1 loaf thinly sliced pumpernickel bread
   Finely chopped chives for garnish

In a mixing bowl, whisk together the Dijon mustard, dry mustard, sugar, white wine, salt, pepper, dill, and horseradish.

Cut the salmon into ½-inch-wide strips. Create rosettes by loosely rolling each strip from one end to the other.

Using a 2-inch round cookie cutter, cut the bread into rounds. Spread each round with the mustard sauce and top with a salmon rosette. Garnish with chopped chives and arrange on a serving platter.

Egg Salad CANAPÉS

Makes 50
hors d'oeuvres

This is a wonderfully refined version of a very commonplace recipe.

12 large eggs, hard-boiled
1 tablespoon minced capers
3 tablespoons grated white radish
2 tablespoons fresh lemon juice
1 scallion, finely chopped, white and green parts
½ teaspoon coarse salt
½ teaspoon freshly ground pepper
1 tablespoon chopped fresh dill
½ teaspoon crushed red pepper flakes
1 loaf thinly sliced light pumpernickel bread
1 red bell pepper, seeded and diced in small squares

In a mixing bowl, chop the eggs with a pastry blender. Stir in the capers, white radish, lemon juice, scallion, salt, pepper, dill, and crushed red pepper and blend until smooth.

Using a 2-inch round cookie or biscuit cutter, cut the bread slices into circles. Spread a tablespoon of egg salad on each round and garnish with a square of red pepper. Arrange on a serving platter.

Index

CONVERSION CHART
Equivalent Imperial and Metric Measurements

American cooks use standard containers, the 8-ounce cup and a tablespoon that takes exactly 16 level fillings to fill that cup level. Measuring by cup makes it very difficult to give weight equivalents, as a cup of densely packed butter will weigh considerably more than a cup of flour. The easiest way therefore to deal with cup measurements in recipes is to take the amount by volume rather than by weight. Thus the equation reads:

1 cup = 240 ml = 8 fl. oz.   ½ cup = 120 ml = 4 fl. oz.

It is possible to buy a set of American cup measures in major stores around the world.
In the United States, butter is often measured in sticks. One stick is the equivalent of 8 tablespoons. One tablespoon of butter is therefore the equivalent to ½ ounce / 15 grams.

LIQUID MEASURES

Fluid ounces	U.S. measures	Imperial measures	Milliliters
	1 TSP	1 TSP	5
¼	2 TSP	1 DESSERTSPOON	7
½	1 TBS	1 TBS	15
1	2 TBS	2 TBS	28
2	¼ CUP	4 TBS	56
4	½ CUP		110
5		¼ PINT or 1 GILL	140
6	¾ CUP		170
8	1 CUP		225
9			250 or ¼ LITER
10	1¼ CUPS	½ PINT	280
12	1½ CUPS		340
15		¾ PINT	420
16	2 CUPS		450
18	2¼ CUPS		500 or ½ LITER
20	2½ CUPS	1 PINT	560
24	3 CUPS		675
25		1¼ PINTS	700
27	3½ CUPS		750
30	3¾ CUPS	1½ PINTS	840
32	4 CUPS		900
35		1¾ PINTS	980
36	4½ CUPS		1000 or 1 LITER
40	5 CUPS	2 PINTS	1120
48	6 CUPS		1350
50		2½ PINTS	1400
60	7½ CUPS		1680
64	8 CUPS		1800
72	9 CUPS		2000 or 2 LITERS
80	10 CUPS	4 PINTS	2250
96	12 CUPS		2700
100		5 PINTS	2800

SOLID MEASURES

U.S. and Imperial Measures		Metric Measures	
Ounces	Pounds	Grams	Kilos
1		28	
2		56	
3 ½		100	
4	¼	112	
5		140	
6		168	
8	½	225	
9		250	¼
12	¾	340	
16	1	450	
18		500	½
20	1¼	560	
24	1½	675	
27		750	¾
28	1¾	780	
32	2	900	
36	2¼	1000	1
40	2½	1100	
48	3	1350	
54		1500	1½
64	4	1800	
72	4½	2000	2
80	5	2250	2¼
90		2500	2½
100	6	2800	2¾

LINEAR MEASURE

1 inch	2.54 centimeters
1 foot	0.3048 meters
1 yard	0.9144 meters
1 mile	1.609 kilometers

AREA MEASURE

1 square inch	6.4516 square centimeters
1 square foot	929.03 square centimeters
1 square yard	0.836 square meters
1 square mile	2.5899 square kilometers

SUGGESTED EQUIVALENTS AND SUBSTITUTES FOR INGREDIENTS

all-purpose flour—plain flour
arugula—rocket
beet—beetroot
coarse salt—kitchen salt
confectioner's sugar—icing sugar
cornstarch—cornflour
eggplant—aubergine
fava beans—broad beans
granulated sugar—caster sugar
lima beans—broad beans
pearl onions—pickling onions
scallion—spring onion
shortening—white fat
snow pea—mangetout
sour cherry—morello cherry
squash—courgettes or marrow
unbleached flour—strong, white flour
vanilla bean—vanilla pod
zest—rind
zucchini—courgettes
light cream—single cream
heavy cream—double cream
half and half—12% fat milk

baking sheet—oven tray
cheesecloth—muslin
parchment paper—greaseproof paper
plastic wrap—cling film

OVEN TEMPERATURE EQUIVALENTS

Fahrenheit	Celsius	Gas Mark	Description
225	110	¼	Cool
250	130	½	
275	140	1	Very Slow
300	150	2	
325	170	3	Slow
350	180	4	Moderate
375	190	5	
400	200	6	Moderately Hot
425	220	7	Fairly Hot
450	230	8	Hot
475	240	9	Very Hot
500	250	10	Extremely Hot

Any broiling recipes can be used with the grill of the oven, but beware of high-temperature grills.